Contents

Fourth-Generation Languages

First published 1987

British Library
Cataloguing in Publication Data
Bate, Joseph St John
    Fourth generation languages under
DOS and UNIX.
    1. DOS (Computer operating system)
    2. UNIX (Computer operating system)
    3. Programming languages (Electronic
        computers)
    I. Title   II. Vadhia, Dinesh B.
    005.4'2   QA76.7

ISBN 0–632–01833–X

BSP Professional Books
Editorial offices:
Osney Mead, Oxford OX2 0EL
    (*Orders*: Tel. 0865 240201)
8 John Street, London WC1N 2ES
23 Ainslie Place, Edinburgh EH3 6AJ
52 Beacon Street, Boston
    Massachusetts 02108, USA
667 Lytton Avenue, Palo Alto
    California 94301, USA
107 Barry Street, Carlton
    Victoria 3053, Australia

Set by V & M Graphics Aylesbury, Bucks
Printed and bound in Great Britain by

Preface

The past few years have seen an explosive growth in the number of installed PCs, based on the industry standard set by IBM using the DOS (MS-DOS and PC-DOS) operating system. In the multi-user arena, after many years of hearing that 'this will be the year of UNIX', UNIX is finally being adopted as a standard. The acceptance of UNIX has occurred largely as a result of user demand rather than through active marketing by traditional computer manufacturers. DOS and UNIX-based computers are increasing continually in performance and capability, and at the same time the costs of these computers are falling dramatically.

Yet despite this great surge in computerisation at the low end of the computer spectrum (in many ways the most effective), the rate at which application software is produced has generally not kept pace with it. This state of affairs, especially in the DP environment, has led to an applications backlog of mammoth proportions. While computer staff struggle to maintain current systems and try to control the backlog, the number of applications required by users increases daily. What is more, today's computer users (increasingly computer-literate through the use of the PC) are requesting applications that are available immediately and that can also cope with the dynamic nature of business in an increasingly competitive economy. The classical system development cycle was never designed to cope with demands like these.

It is within this scenario that a revolution is taking place in computer languages and the way in which application software is being developed. The changes that have come about over the past few years point to a time, in the foreseeable future, when the majority of business-oriented systems will be developed using these fourth-generation languages (4GLs).

The first part of the book sets out the advantages of the fourth-generation environment and the role played by DOS and UNIX. Approaches to prototyping are also covered. As part of the fourth-generation application development cycle, prototyping addresses the problem of continually changing user requirements. The second half of the book provides more detail about specific areas, including DOS, UNIX, databases, relational database management systems and commercially available fourth-generation languages.

In the course of this book we mention a number of software packages, but these represent only a small proportion of the fourth-generation languages available for DOS and UNIX-based computers. If we do not mention a package, this does not mean that it is not worthy of further examination. Moreover, as fourth-generation languages are constantly being improved and upgraded and new ones are also being introduced, a definitive study would soon be out of date.

This book was written using two word-processing packages on various DOS-based computers (Superwriter on the Apricot and Wordstar on the IBM PC, DEC Rainbow 100 and Amstrad 1512). The diagrams were designed and produced on an Apple Macintosh system, with unfailing guidance and support from Kirty Wilson-Davies, a desktop publishing expert. We would also like to thank all those friends, colleagues and organisations who helped us in our research and preliminary work, and acknowledge the useful material provided in James Martin's book *Fourth Generation Languages* (published by Prentice-Hall).

We have both worked in various capacities at a leading systems house on the development of systems using fourth-generation languages under DOS and UNIX. During that time we witnessed a large number of system implementations from which we learnt a great deal. We hope that this book will help you to profit from the opportunities and benefits to be derived through the use of 4GLs.

Trademark Acknowledgements

IBM is a registered trademark of International Business Machines Corporation.
PC-DOS, OS/2 and SQL are trademarks of International Business Machines Corporation.
Ingres is a registered trademark of Relational Technology.
Accell and Unify are registered trademarks of Unify Corporation.
Informix is a registered trademark of Informix Inc.
Oracle and SDD are registered trademarks of Oracle Corporation.
UNIX is a registered trademark of AT&T Bell Laboratories.
MS-DOS, Windows and Xenix are trademarks of Microsoft Corporation.
dBase is a trademark of Ashton Tate Corporation.
Lotus and 1-2-3 are trademarks of Lotus Development Corporation.
DEC, VAX, VMS and ULTRIX are trademarks of Digital Equipment Corporation.

Joseph St John Bate
Dinesh B. Vadhia

Part 1. The Fourth-Generation Environment

Chapter One
The Application Software Crisis

The power of today's computing technology is awesome; however, it is not being used as effectively as it could in many organisations and corporations. Data processing is bogged down in problems, the majority of them associated with traditional methods, languages and the mainframe mentality. A great number of these problems can be resolved by the use of PCs and UNIX-based supermicros and an appropriate fourth generation language.

The computer is a flexible machine – DP departments are not

The computer is one of the most flexible machines ever invented, capable of a staggering diversity of applications. It is rapidly dropping in cost, and if used properly its ever-increasing power can improve the efficiency of any organisation. The problem lies not in the machine itself, but in the method used for creating applications. The traditional application development life-cycle is slow and rigid; the methods have been 'cast in concrete' in many organisations' standards and procedures. But the procedures are not working for the systems required by the users. This inability to use computers effectively should be regarded as a major organisational problem to which solutions must be found. The problem has now reached crisis proportions for some organisations – and their ability to compete in their market place is suffering.

Constant demand for new applications

Even in most well-managed corporations the demand for new applications is rising faster than DP departments can supply them. The imbalance between demand and supply is steadily becoming worse, and the user is the one who suffers. The backlog of needed applications is growing to such an extent that most corporations now have a documented backlog of two to four years. In some extreme cases the backlog is as long as seven years. This situation is likely to deteriorate as machines drop in price and become available to more and more potential users; unless, that is, better methods of creating applications are found and used.

Long backlogs and the inability of computer departments to respond to users' needs quickly are very frustrating for the user and detrimental to the health of the organisation. In some cases the users have taken the law into their own hands and brought computer expertise into their own department instead of relying on internal DP resources. This is not always the most efficient use of resources, since it prevents the whole organisation from functioning as an entity.

An invisible backlog

Although today's application backlogs are long they reveal another, more sinister problem. When the documented backlog is as long as several years, the users do not even consider asking for many of the applications that they need. There is therefore an *invisible* backlog. This invisible backlog cannot easily be measured. What *can* be measured is the continuing demand for personal computers and associated software. In other words, users who need applications that would be valuable to them and profitable to their organisation do not ask for them because of the DP overload.

DP staff spend their time on maintenance

The problems of DP personnel and software development are made worse by the maintenance problem. The term 'maintenance' refers to the restructuring and rewriting of existing systems to accommodate new requirements or to make them work with changed system resources. Reprogramming is often needed because separate development programs do not fit together, or because interface problems exist when data is passed from one system to another. A necessary change in one program sets off a whole chain reaction of changes that have to be made in other programs. If not consciously minimised, maintenance tends to rise as the number of programs grows. The interaction among programs grows roughly as the square of the number of programs unless it is deliberately controlled. Another problem is the time spent looking for and then fixing bugs in software that has been poorly documented.

The maintenance burden hinders the growing number of applications required from being implemented. The maintenance activity in some DP departments consumes up to 75% of the total personnel resource.

US government figures indicate that the Department of Defense spent $2

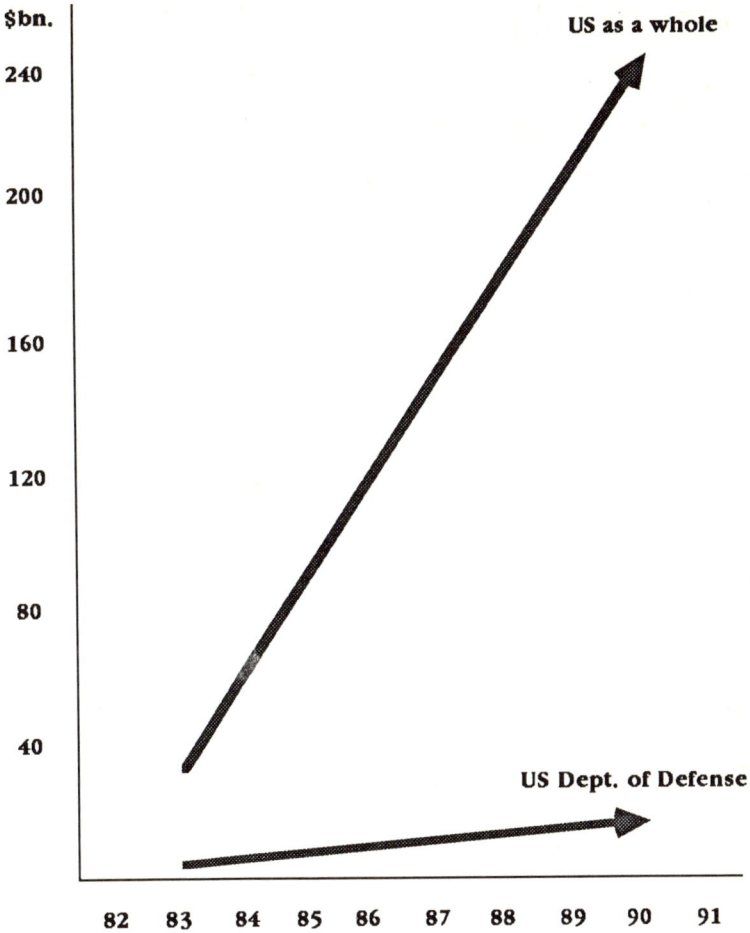

, *Fig. 1.1* US software maintenance costs (actual and linear projected).

billion on software maintenance in 1983, and estimates that it will rise to $16 billion by the end of the 1980s. The United States as a whole was thought to be spending $30 billion per year on maintenance in 1983. It would be economically catastrophic if the figure for 1990 rose by the same ratio. For those who think that the UK is immune, the figures for the UK are roughly proportional. It is statistics like these, and the continual demand for ever more applications, that has led to the 'software crisis' that we are now suffering. It is crucial from an organisational and financial point of view that all efforts are made to reduce the cost of maintenance.

Redefining the work pattern

Systems analysts and other non-programmers often think that existing programs which are working can be left alone. In reality the data that most programs create or use is needed for other applications, and is almost always needed in a slightly different form. The maintenance mess has become a nightmare in some corporations and a matter of concern to all organisations. It is alarming to reflect what the situation could be like in 20 years' time, especially if more and more applications and systems are added using conventional methodology. Either the whole system will grind to a halt or most of the adult population will be employed in maintaining programs! It is not a happy situation for any managing director or company chairman to contemplate.

Today, because of the backlog caused by the use of low-level application development techniques, many DP managers perceive the pressure from users for applications as excessive. In reality, however, most users have barely begun to realise the potential of computing for improving their productivity and their companies' profitability. The pressure will increase. This growing demand for applications and the shortage of programmers will be a powerful reason for user-creative computing.

There is one more powerful reason for the trend towards end-user computing. In many situations the conventional application development process does not work. Time and time again one hears of a system being cut after years of development effort. Alternatively, when it finally arrives after months of work by DP departments the end users say it is not what they wanted, or try it for a while and then discard it. The common reaction to this situation is to say that the requirements were not specified thoroughly enough. As a result, even more elaborate procedures have to be devised for requirement specification. This results in huge documentation, but the system is still seen to be unsatisfactory.

Understanding what the user wants is not an exact science

Most users of DP resources do not know what they want until they have experienced using the system. Often the user's first experience of a new system highlights the uncomfortable fact that many changes are needed to make it meet their basic requirements. Programming is not an exact science, nor is understanding what the user wants. The DP department forgets this at their peril. A system is a living organism, and the users will help it grow. Once the users are comfortable with the system, their imagination goes to work. They think of all sorts of different functions and variations that would be useful to them, and quite naturally they want these changes incorporated, usually immediately. DP departments often say that as soon as they have designed and built the perfect system the user wants to change it. This is a reflection of human nature and the dynamic nature of business.

DP personnel are thinking people

Many DP organisations have realised that their application creation process is not working to the satisfaction of the user and have taken steps to correct it. Unfortunately, the steps that are often taken result in a worsening situation. This is because they are usually designed to enforce formal procedures for specifying requirements. The argument put forward is that application development must be converted from a sloppy ad hoc operation to one following rigid rules, like an engineering discipline. This formal approach can work well if, and only if, the user requirements can be specified in fine detail *before* design and programming begin. With certain systems they can, but with the majority they cannot. For instance, the requirements for production control can be specified completely beforehand, but those for management information systems (MIS) cannot. Almost every attempt to do so has failed and will continue to fail. Management information systems require a basic core of business information, but companies, like people, are different, and their MIS requirements are also different.

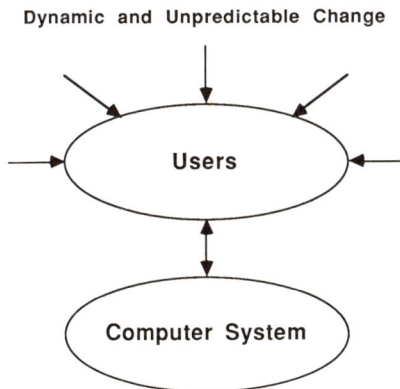

Fig. 1.2 Computer systems must respond quickly to changing user needs.

In a commercial environment the requirements of most systems change as soon as the executive starts to use his terminal. They also change as and when the business develops. Commercial organisations exist in an environment of constant dynamic and unpredictable change, and executives have to operate in this environment. Because of this the requirements for computer systems cannot be predicted with any accuracy. For some systems pre-determined specifications are about as realistic as trying to predict the weather a month in advance. The classical development life-cycle does succeed for certain types of system. For others it does not work, and any attempt to enforce it makes it impossible to obtain the results that are needed. In many cases DP personnel would understand the differences between the various types of system if they understood how organisations worked, especially the one for which they work.

Management information systems and the DP department

Despite repeated failures, management information systems are one of the most important classes of data processing and one that *can* contribute to the well-being of an organisation. Using the traditional development approach, the MIS designer will go to the manager and ask what information he would like to look at. After long and painful experience it seems that most managers do not really know what information they need.

The MIS designer must be aware of the types of decision a manager will or should make and how he will make them. Some executives play safe and ask for everything. In response to these demands, some designers have tried to *provide* everything on large reports that tend to hide rather than reveal the few pieces of information that are really required. In some cases an executive with a strong personality makes firm statements about the information that the department wants. A systems analyst at last receives a clear directive and an unambiguous statement of requirements is created. However, time rolls on, and by the time the programming and testing are complete the executive in question has moved on. His replacement doesn't like the system. Such a system is inevitably highly personalised and hardly ever survives the departure of the original user.

Ad hoc is often better

The types of system for which pre-specified computing does not work are becoming more and more important in running corporations. A more ad hoc approach is replacing the classical life-cycle. It is characterised by quick and easy building of prototypes or applications, which can be quickly modified. It relies on interactive application building and step by step refinement of the results.

User-driven computing and pre-specified computing

It is, then, necessary to distinguish between systems that need dynamic modification of requirements after the system is installed and systems that need complete, formal requirements, analysis and specification before implementation. These are called *user-driven computing* and *pre-specified computing* respectively, and all application developments ought to be categorised as one or the other. Each requires entirely different techniques and management.

Unfortunately a lot of computing that ought to be user-driven is being developed as if it were pre-specified computing. Much commercial administrative data processing falls into the user-driven category, and so do systems oriented to human needs. Their development requires a technique that allows for trial and error. This type of development is not appropriate for highly complex technical systems, such as those for refinery operations, satellite image processing, air traffic control, or rocket launchers. These demand a very precise requirement specification and a formal development life-cycle with tight controls. It is for such complex and critical systems that the Ada language has been developed.

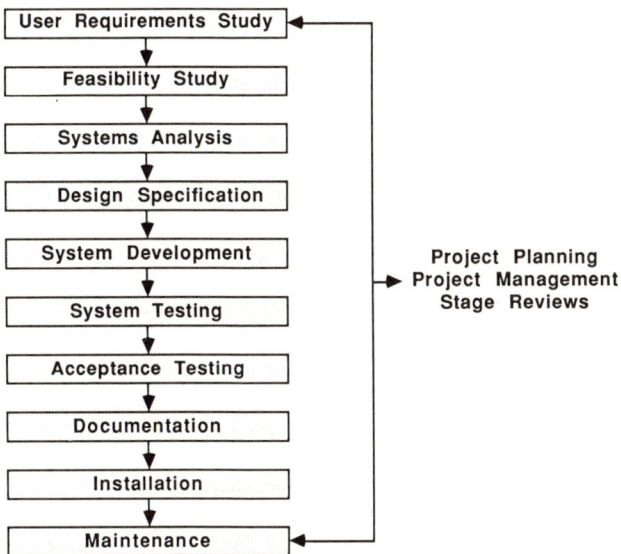

```
┌──────────────────────────┐
│ User Requirements Study  │◄──────┐
└──────────────────────────┘       │
           ↓                        │
┌──────────────────────────┐       │
│     Feasibility Study     │      │
└──────────────────────────┘       │
           ↓                        │
┌──────────────────────────┐       │
│     Systems Analysis      │      │
└──────────────────────────┘       │
           ↓                        │
┌──────────────────────────┐       │
│   Design Specification    │      │
└──────────────────────────┘       │         Project Planning
           ↓                        │      ► Project Management
┌──────────────────────────┐       │         Stage Reviews
│    System Development     │      │
└──────────────────────────┘       │
           ↓                        │
┌──────────────────────────┐       │
│      System Testing       │      │
└──────────────────────────┘       │
           ↓                        │
┌──────────────────────────┐       │
│    Acceptance Testing     │      │
└──────────────────────────┘       │
           ↓                        │
┌──────────────────────────┐       │
│      Documentation        │      │
└──────────────────────────┘       │
           ↓                        │
┌──────────────────────────┐       │
│       Installation        │      │
└──────────────────────────┘       │
           ↓                        │
┌──────────────────────────┐       │
│       Maintenance         │◄──────┘
└──────────────────────────┘
```

Fig. 1.3   The classical software application development life-cycle.

The classical software development life-cycle

To achieve a successful implementation the classical software development life-cycle demands:

- **User requirement study** (determines user needs for an application).

- **Feasibility study** (determines the technical and economic feasibility of developing the application).

- **Systems analysis** (produces a 'functional specification' in business terms). This document serves as the basis for user agreement on the facilities to be provided. Systems analysis is composed of *requirement analysis, data analysis* and *functional analysis.*

- **Design specification** (transforms the logical view of the application into a physical specification of programs, files, inputs, outputs and controls). The primary objective of the design stage is to ensure that the application will be easy to maintain taking performance targets and hardware characteristics into account.

- **System development** (produces programs from the specifications documented at the design stage). This involves detailed program specification (pseudo-code), coding, testing of program modules, and program documentation.

- **System testing** (demonstrates the reliability of the application as a whole).

- **Acceptance testing** (ensures that the application meets the user's requirement).

- **Documentation for users** (aids the user in the operation of the application).

- **Installation** and **training of users** ('going live').

- **Maintenance** (modifying the application software during operation).

Two points should be noted about the development life-cycle:

- It is clear from the very start what the system will do; there is no incremental development.

- The user sees the finished application and results only at the very end of the cycle.

Problems with the classical development life-cycle

When applied to user-driven applications, the classical development life-cycle is too slow and too expensive, and the user requirements analysis is too formal and concrete. Traditional methods are are not flexible enough to address the continually changing requirements of the user. Changes are often needed in a day, not a year, and must be made as and when required.

In order to develop commercial applications using third-generation languages (3GLs) vast numbers of lines of code are needed. These languages were designed for DP professionals rather than users. It was and still is time-consuming to debug them, and the modification of complex systems is equally time-consuming, laborious and difficult. Many DP departments become bogged down in the complexities associated with third-generation languages. This often means they cannot respond to business needs as quickly as they should, which leads to a continual backlog of unsatisfied user demand for computer applications. It was this user frustration that was exploited by the personal computer.

Demand for bespoke applications continues

It is five years since the IBM PC was introduced, and it is interesting to quote from a recent US survey on users and PC software – off-the-shelf, customised and bespoke applications.

Within the US corporate and institutional organisations 80% of software used on PCs is off-the-shelf. However, more and more users are demanding customisation or bespoke solutions to meet their needs more adequately. One out of every five applications used within an organisation has either been customised for the user or developed from scratch. Customised software accounts for 6% and bespoke for 14% of the total number of applications.

Among the users practically everyone used at least one off-the-shelf package. Of these, 31% customised software packages themselves and 20% had packages customised either by the manufacturer or a third party. The most astounding result from the survey is that 62% of users have bespoke

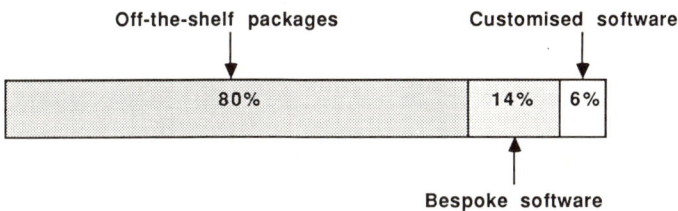

Fig. 1.4 Application software types within US organisations.

applications developed from within the organisation and 29% from third parties, i.e. systems houses.

Fourth-generation languages are the way forward

To satisfy this voracious appetite for ever more applications the only way forward is with the aid of 4GLs. They can provide the productivity rises necessary to sustain the users' hunger.

Chapter Two
End-user Computing, Common Operating Systems and Fourth-Generation Languages

The computer has left the closed sanctum where it was once guarded by the druids of the DP department. It is now on the desks of end users – the knowledge workers of the information age. Figures for 1986 show that in the UK the value of personal computers sold now exceeds that of mainframes. This trend will continue. We have entered a new and exciting stage in the development of the information age, which is merging computer power with the needs of commerce and industry.

In the coming years user-driven computing, using personal computers and supermicros, will become a major factor. Users have begun to rely on computer power to improve their productivity, and the profitability and effectiveness of their companies. Users are becoming computer literate. They know what they want and those who ignore this development do so at their peril.

Traditional methods will become redundant

It is equally certain that DP departments employing traditional computing methods and third-generation languages (COBOL, C, Pascal, PL/1, BASIC, FORTRAN) will become redundant. The reason is simple. The combination of traditional methods and traditional DP departments is failing to satisfy the commercial requirements of the '80s; the situation can only worsen in the '90s unless radical changes take place. In short, they have failed. They are not flexible enough and they are too costly. They are not suitable for developing many of the systems required by the knowledge workers as they wrestle to ensure their companies' viability in this increasingly competitive society.

An evolutionary jump is taking place in the computer industry. In the mainframe environment there was a need for specialised personnel to program and operate the machines. In the age of personal computing everyone has to become programmer and operator. This is the market area that fourth-generation languages aim to serve. They will open the hitherto exclusive systems analysis and programming environment to every user.

The challenge of making the knowledge worker productive

The two most evident impacts upon society in this century have been made by the motor car and the computer. Today over 80% of the population between the ages of 18 and 65 know how to drive a car, but less than 10% know how to operate a computer. Cars and lifestyles are closely linked; computers and lifestyles will become linked in the same way. The results will soon become apparent to information system professionals and users. The quickest and most efficient method of driving these personal computers and supermicros will be with productivity tools such as fourth-generation languages – not by using out-of-date traditional methodologies. The knowledge worker needs decisive help, not hindrance.

Definition of 'knowledge work'

The introduction of the personal computer as a workstation has forced management to examine the way in which the most highly paid executives work. This examination has taken place in an effort to improve their productivity by using personal computing. Statistics show that before the introduction of the PC productive 'knowledge' work accounted for approximately 33% of an executive's time. The rest was spent on administration and unproductive activities. The aim of most profitable and well-managed companies is to reverse these figures. When this comes about, executives will become 'knowledge workers' and not administrative personnel.

Knowledge work is not easily definable. The term contrasts with manual work, physical production work or physical service work. Knowledge work is based on the knowledge possessed by the worker not on the ability to perform physical tasks. The output of knowledge work includes diagnoses, descriptions, instructions, schedules, plans, memoranda, reports, papers, decisions etc. By way of contrast, the output of physical production work is a physical product (a ton of coal, silicon chips, etc.) or a physical service (window cleaning, car servicing, etc.)

Knowledge work involves thinking

A useful definition of knowledge work is that it involves thinking, processing information, and formulating analyses, recommendations and procedures.

a) **Without Computers and 4GL s**

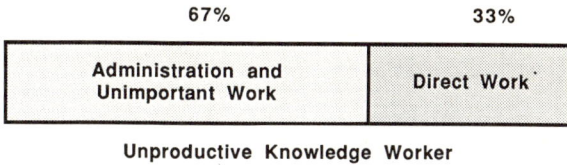

67%   33%

Administration and Unimportant Work	Direct Work

Unproductive Knowledge Worker

b) **With Computers and 4GL s**

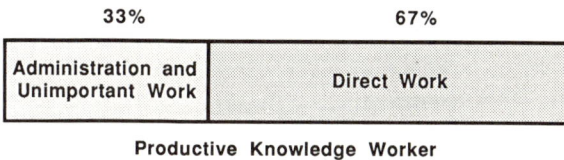

33%   67%

Administration and Unimportant Work	Direct Work

Productive Knowledge Worker

Fig. 2.1   Distribution of 'Knowledge Work' for executives.

Knowledge work may use verbal or written inputs and outputs. Knowledge work tasks involve the use of information. Some of this information derives from the knowledge and expertise of the knowledge worker; the rest from organisational and external data to which the knowledge worker has access.

Knowledge work is a relative concept. There are knowledge work components in many tasks, and there are probably no jobs exclusively composed of knowledge work or lacking knowledge work altogether. A person in a clerical position with highly structured, routine tasks may have relatively little knowledge work, but some clerical jobs involve significant amounts of knowledge work; most managerial activities have high levels of knowledge work, but managers also perform tasks that have little.

Easily programmed computers are productivity tools for knowledge workers

Computers are productivity tools for the knowledge worker, provided they can be programmed quickly, easily and in accordance with the worker's requirements. As managers and other users grow more conversant with computers and communications, they will resent receiving information that has been regulated by someone else's perception of their needs. They want to make their own decisions about the rate, shape, format, content, layout and delivery of that information. The software associated with the computer must enable users to style their own information needs. This user need highlights some of the problems faced by the traditional DP manager.

DP managers face problems

The problem facing many DP managers is that they are not satisfying the needs of the managers. Managers are not receiving the information they require from existing computer systems. Decisions that should be made with the aid of computers are in fact being made using traditional methods, or with inadequate information; or worse still, with *inaccurate* information. In many cases this is because the systems have been developed using traditional technology and third-generation languages. Such systems, by their very nature and design, are so difficult to change that they inhibit the implementation of the new and important systems urgently required in the competitive market place. This has resulted in users becoming increasingly hostile towards DP departments. They feel powerless. But they will not be powerless very much longer.

Top managers are angry that the resources spent on computing in the form of hardware, software, manpower, skills training, maintenance and support increase yearly, yet seem unable to change procedures to give them the information they require. In one corporation with an expensive and elegant world-wide computer network, the chief executive complained bitterly that for years he had been asking for daily or even weekly figures of cash balances. He seemed no nearer to obtaining them than he would have been in an organisation run using paper documents and conventional filing systems. This is by no means an isolated case. Here are some common criticisms of in-house DP departments made by users and senior management.

(1) Users do not obtain applications when they want them. There is always a delay, sometimes of years.
(2) It is difficult or impossible to make the changes that management require to reflect the changes in the commercial environment.
(3) The systems show up errors after installation. This causes frustration, time delays and, more importantly, financial loss.
(4) The systems delivered rarely match the users' true requirements. A major problem is that DP staff provide systems they think the user should have, rather than providing systems the user wants.
(5) It is difficult to communicate precise requirements to DP personnel, owing to their lack of commercial awareness or even interest.
(6) The specifications which users have to agree and sign for are lengthy and difficult to check. More often than not, they are also impossible to understand.

(7) System development and maintenance costs usually overshoot the anticipated budget. This is because DP managers underestimate the development timescale and use inefficient and ineffective methodologies.
(8) The lead time to develop systems is so long that many immediate and important support systems are never implemented. This invariably loses the company business opportunities.
(9) The majority of DP staff are involved in the maintenance and enhancement of systems that are crumbling at the edges because of poor design, badly written code and non-existent documentation.

These are devastating criticisms, and many come from users and management belonging to major organisations. This state of affairs has been going on for years, and it was into this environment that the personal computer was launched. The result was that the personal computer and its associated software (for example Lotus 123 and dBase II and III) became a runaway success almost overnight. This was at a time when the personal computer had very limited power. The DP department might have laughed at the first personal computers and called them toys, but as far as the user was concerned they worked – which was more than could be said for some DP departments. The personal computer is increasing in power and capability dramatically, as are the available software development tools. The user now demands the best – and quickly. Can the DP department respond, or will the users continue to take the initiative?

Personal computer starts a new trend

The grey box containing the IBM Personal Computer has changed the face of the commercial world to an extent few can imagine. This change has been hastened by the introduction of the many PC clones, not least the Amstrad 1512. It has provided low-priced and powerful computing, and the majority of users have taken to it like ducks to water.

It was not the personal computer hardware that was the most innovative element in this revolution, but the software, and Lotus 123 in particular. This package gave the users (many of whom had never seen a computer before, let alone used one) the ability to be productive after a few days' training. The way in which first-time computer users developed systems using Lotus 123 and other spreadsheets should be an inspiration to all those who are apprehensive about developing systems using 4GLs for the first time.

The speadsheet has a number of attributes associated with a 4GL. Lotus 123 and comparable products were designed from the outset to satisfy the needs of users, and as such included those facilities which were required. End users could be productive with one to two days' training, and they did not require special computing knowledge. As a result, systems were developed without the need to understand and learn a complex third-generation language. Even so, the range of 4GLs that will come on to the market to exploit the new IBM operating system OS/2 and hardware based on the Intel 386 chip will make the current spreadsheets appear timid by comparison. However, the spreadsheet will continue to be one of the most widely-used computer productivity tools for a number of years to come.

The personal computer market is maturing

A major force behind the increased demand has been the maturing of the personal computer software marketplace. Those who develop their own applications using personal computers, like software developers, have found the going difficult. They are faced with problems similar to those that confront the DP manager; higher user demands, stiffer competition, and increasing salaries for professional programmers. The total cost of developing quality application products has grown substantially. Meanwhile the level of competition has also increased. It is no longer enough just to have a good product idea, as was the case in the early days of personal computer development. Now the developer must get to the market in a timely fashion with effective promotion if he is to have any chance of success.

Personal computer users who require these products face a difficult dilemma. Even when they can find quality software, often none of the available products exactly meets their needs. The demands that have to be satisfied in a mature market are more complex. This also reflects the change in individual needs within the organisation. When personal computers first became available, anything was better than nothing as far as the user was concerned.

Why live with an imperfect fit?

Users, then, must either live with a standard package that comes close enough to their needs or build their own application. Sometimes their needs are uncomplicated – a simple invoicing application, for instance. More often, however, these users (especially knowledge workers) are faced with a problem for which they cannot buy software and have no alternative but to write their own. Not long ago, users who decided to build their own system were faced with the prospect of having to learn a traditional language such as COBOL or BASIC. Some users did so successfully, but for many the result was both costly and unsatisfactory. Others made do with what they could buy. The majority did nothing.

Developing quality applications using a third-generation language is far too long a process for most knowledge workers. The little time they have must be spent carrying out their professional tasks. If outside DP resources are used, the results are invariably the same as using internal DP resources. By the time the application is completed, the needs of the user will have changed. Worse still, the person who developed the application may leave, causing even greater delay. The cost of application development does not end with the initial development. Often more resources are expended maintaining an application than were used to build it. The requirements placed on the application will change over time. Programs written in 3GLs are typically very costly to update and maintain. This is because of the vast number of lines of code that are used and the problems of interrelationships. Users will often settle for what they already have rather than try to change the application to match their changing needs, simply because of the cost and pain of change. However, in the new, fast-moving commercial environment of the late '80s and '90s this will be unacceptable.

Problems facing the personal computer user and software developer are the same

The basic problems facing knowledge workers who use intelligent terminals and professional application developers are very similar. They all boil down to a need for tools that enable them to build maintainable applications more quickly and with fewer skills. In other words, they want tools that make them more productive than they would be if they were programming in traditional languages. The answer lies in the use of 'standard components': a builder uses standard parts when building a house, and would certainly never think of designing each part from scratch.

This theme unites all the packages that are grouped together under the 4GL banner. All are designed to make the people who use them more productive. However, their approach to this goal varies widely. The easiest way to categorise these products is by their goals and their primary market. Some, such as Ashton Tate's dBase III, are designed to be complete replacements for traditional programming languages. Products such as these are often called *application generators.*

Application generators are aimed at the intelligent personal computer user and professional application developers. They are not intended to address any single problem area. Instead they are are meant to be used to implement a broad range of applications. Often these applications will be distributed within an organisation or industry for general use. It is therefore important that standard hardware and operating systems are available.

Users will continue to look for computer power that they can control. The development of 4GLs both for the personal computer and for UNIX multi-user systems will provide the tools that the users require. With these productivity tools, users will have the power to resolve many of their problems and will expect the DP departments to do likewise.

The first three generations of computer languages

To understand the importance of fourth-generation languages, it will help to trace the development of computer languages.

The first generation of computer languages were centred on machine code instructions. These early computers were programmed directly in the binary digits of the machines' operating codes. However, since machine code is intimately tied to a particular hardware architecture, programming required specialised and thorough knowledge of a machine. Bit level programming was very time consuming and prone to error.

The second generation of languages were the symbolic assembler languages that came into use in the mid 1950s. Assembly languages provide an alphabetic mnemonic code for each machine instruction, facilitating easier development and understanding of programs. Again, assembler languages were closely tied to the hardware architecture and thus did not provide any form of portability between different manufacturers' hardware. Assembly language programming was not something that users could pick up, and was left to programmers with an intimate knowledge of the hardware. Not

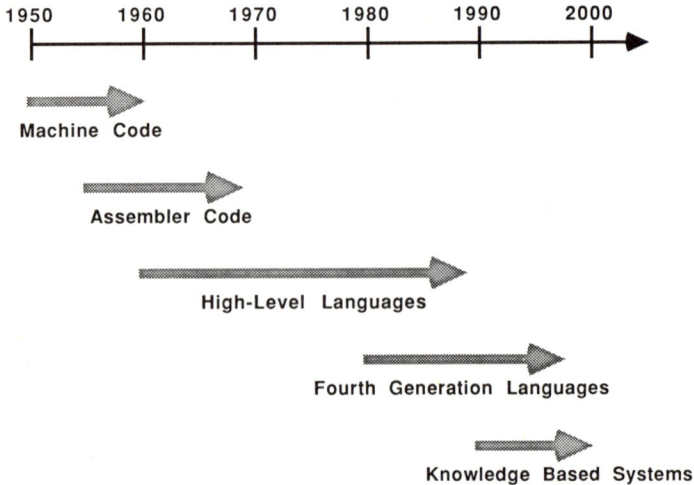

Fig. 2.2 Language types since 1950.

surprisingly, they were treated as a cross between magicians and priests.

Third generation languages came into use in the 1960s and were procedurally oriented. The first, FORTRAN, was developed by IBM and aimed specifically at scientists and engineers. It was closely followed by COBOL, whose development was initiated by the US Navy and was primarily designed to serve the needs of commerce. These languages were termed 'higher-level' since they provided an interface between the programmer and the native machine instructions. The higher-level languages led to the design of structured high-level languages (such as Pascal, C, and PL/1) which provided constructs that enabled programmers to write code in a uniformly structured fashion. However, for commercial applications COBOL became by far the most commonly used computer language.

Third-generation languages become hardware independent

The use of third-generation languages meant that software development became to a large extent independent of the hardware. Using these languages, programs could be coded without any knowledge of the machine instruction set and registers, although programmers needed some knowledge of the machine if they wished to optimise execution efficiency. It was because of this hardware independence that programs could be converted, with a greater or lesser degree of difficulty, to run on different machines. This led to the creation of manufacture-independent standards for third-generation languages, but notwithstanding these developments, the portability of programs still presented problems. In many respects it was more a concept than a reality, but portability is important because it helps to protect the software development investment and provide machine independence.

Industry standard operating systems give power to the user

An important factor in the success of the personal computer has been the operating system introduced by IBM. PC-DOS/MS-DOS, usually referred to generically as DOS, has become the 'de facto' industry standard for single-user intelligent workstations. Once, every personal computer manufacturer had a different operating system, different sized disks, etc. leading to incompatibility with everything else – including systems in their own range. The ACT Apricot range was a classic example of how to muddle the consumer and lose market share by making every machine in the range incompatible with every other. The user has demanded a standard. It has come about because of market forces and not because established computer

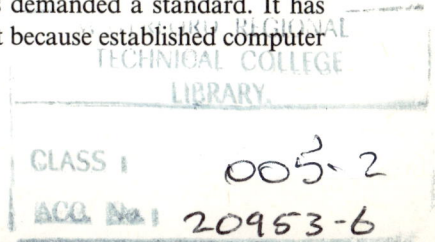

companies have been allowed to agree between themselves what should or should not be a standard.

DOS as a standard has encouraged new entrants into the personal computer market by offering low price, high quality products. In the UK, Amstrad is a prime example, providing high quality DOS-based personal computers at a fraction of the price charged by traditional computer manufacturers. DOS has also given software producers the opportunity to reach a wider market with inexpensive application and development software. This has resulted in a wealth of software of exceptional quality becoming available, again at a fraction of the cost of mainframe and mini software. IBMs original endorsement has led to a standard that is available worldwide. It is likely that market forces will decide that it is time to have an industry standard for multi-user supermicros.

Computer users, having benefited from an industry standard operating system in the single user arena are asking if it is possible to have a standard operating system for multi-user computers. If this were left to the major computer manufacturers we could wait until kingdom come and be no further forward. It is not in the interests of traditional computer companies to have 'industry standards' – the consumer is the only person to benefit.

Operating system portability

The primary benefit of an industry standard operating system is portability of applications, permitting the organisation to save the investment in its software. It also allows advantage to be taken of new developments in hardware design and capability from a wide range of suppliers. This, however, calls for portability of system calls, very high level programming tools, and utilities and applications designed to meet information processing needs in a machine independent form.

It is through programming portability that system enhancements as major as replacing a CPU or as minor as upgrading a printer can easily be dealt with. At a time when hardware designs proliferate, an operating system which is hardware-independent is a necessity. The operating system must also offer protocols and utilities to satisfy the growing demand for communications.

UNIX as a standard multi-user operating system

There are two keys to operating systems gaining acceptance as the 'de facto' standard. The first is enthusiastic support from hardware manufacturers. The second is the availability of a wide range of application software. UNIX answers the first criterion well, although in application's software it is still lagging behind DOS. The new and powerful range of 4GL offerings under UNIX has resulted in this gap closing.

The support that UNIX has on user premises, the training of a population of information scientists in its features, and the support of almost all hardware manufacturers, has ensured that UNIX has a life expectancy that will last well into the next century. How many other multi-user operating systems can say the same? One reason the UNIX system is evolving so rapidly as a viable entity in the industry is that it is a mature and stable operating system.

All chips lead to UNIX

The broadest implementation market for UNIX is the supermicro, based primarily on the Motorola 680X0, Intel 286 and 386 families of microprocessors. However, UNIX has also been successfully ported onto a wide range of 32-bit machines up to mainframes. The AT&T subsidiary Western Electric designed the WE320X0 microprocessor family specifically to optimise UNIX. A new AT&T policy is now in the making. Apart from having signed UNIX for their VLSI, chip manufacturers will have to have their microprocessors and their version of UNIX certified by Western Electric. As AT&T has suggested, if chips and operating systems are certified then the applications will be portable.

At the same time the trend to UNIX is gaining momentum. Even manufacturers who resisted UNIX have been forced to adopt it by market pressures. After trying for years to oppose the proliferation of UNIX, DEC finally announced support for it. The same is the case for IBM, via its 6150 computer and AIX.

The stability that these moves have given the UNIX marketplace has encouraged software developers to launch new and exciting productivity tools.

Definition of fourth-generation languages

There are a number of definitions of fourth-generation languages. Some provide a list of all the features they should possess, others define them by what they achieve, while some authorities offer a formal definition in terms that it is almost impossible to understand.

We prefer to define a fourth-generation language as 'a productivity tool for the rapid development of software applications.' In other words, they are tools that do not require recourse to the lengthy and formal methods associated with 3GLs. Specifically, they describe and implement *what is to be done*, and not *how it is to be done* by a computer.

A wide range of offerings fall under this heading, including:

- Database management systems (DBMS)
- Query languages
- Report generators
- Interactive business graphics
- Integrated software packages

There is a niche in the computing environment of today and tomorrow for each one of these 4GLs. Some appeal to simple problems, others to complex problems and larger machines. What ties them together is the new outlook necessary for their use and the tremendous productivity gains that can be obtained. These productivity tools are the major component of the fourth generation environment (4GE).

A radical change in approach is required

Fourth-generation languages require change in the conventional software development procedures, which are largely based on the characteristics of third-generation languages. Without radically new development cycles, the use of 4GLs will produce only a marginal payoff, if any at all. 4GLs are a new way of looking at application development.

We should look at 4GLs not as a problem but as an opportunity. We should remember that there are plenty of examples to demonstrate that avoiding problems by avoiding change leads logically to an even more absurd conclusion: avoiding the solution of problems by avoiding the use of high technology. The use of new technology has been and always will be the only way forward.

Be lean and mean to survive

Old technology gives a comparatively poor return on investment. Computer power must support the human elements rather than bureacracy and organisational red tape. Project teams must be agile, lean and small. Advanced development and support tools should be evaluated and used as soon as they become available.

In order to survive in the current and future competitive market, information systems are a prerequisite; however, clearly defined goals and objectives have to be set to ensure success. There is a need to study workflow, to simplify and consolidate established productivity ratios, and to identify priority areas which can be rationalised through computers and communications. Those who take advantage of the 4GE will survive to be ready for the fifth generation.

Beyond the fourth comes the fifth

It is useful to have an understanding of fifth-generation languages in order to appreciate the offerings that will be available in the near future. Many of these will be available on personal computers, since they will be aimed at the knowledge worker. The term 'fifth generation' usually refers to systems that use disciplines originating in the field of artificial intelligence, especially:

- Knowledge-based systems
- Expert systems
- Inference engines
- Processing of human languages

A fifth-generation system encodes complex knowledge so that a user may draw inferences from it. In some cases, this inference processing is used to perform tasks that, although complex, seem trivial to humans, such as understanding speech, vision, and human language. In other cases, the fast processing of inferences that are not instinctive to humans makes the software appear to be highly intelligent. In highly specialised areas of knowledge, the system can display an apparent expertise far greater than most humans.

Languages designed for these areas may be described as fifth-generation languages. In order that fifth generation languages should have the necessary processing power available to exploit their capabilities, fifth-generation computers in the future are likely to employ parallel processors. This is because it is economically desirable to have many mass-produced processors working on a problem simultaneously. Languages designed for highly parallel computing will emerge to exploit this technology.

3GLs are vanity, 4GLs are sanity

There is a saying within business circles that 'turnover is vanity, profit is sanity'; the same philosophy may be applied to 3GLs and 4GLs. Now is the time to set the wheels in motion to ensure success. Fourth-generation languages present an opportunity not to be ignored. The 4GLs will be followed by the fifth generation of intelligent systems; but first we must profit effectively from the fourth generation.

> # 3GLs are VANITY,
> # 4GLs are SANITY

Fig. 2.3   A saying to keep in mind.

Chapter Three
Introduction to Fourth-Generation Languages

A change is taking place in computer languages, a change that is long overdue. There is a user-led demand to be able to develop application software much more easily and quickly than in the past. There are two main reasons for this. First, the number of computer installations is increasing rapidly, and at the same time the raw processing power and storage available is decreasing in cost dramatically.

Computers will increase in speed and power, with DOS- and UNIX-based machines continuing to spread rapidly. The silicon factories from both east and west will continue to compete against each other to produce chips that are cheaper and more powerful in terms of processing power and memory. Soon there will be many millions of personal computers, some of which will be as powerful as mainframes ten years previously. Users can purchase computers quickly and easily; now they now want application software developed quickly and easily. It is the responsibility of the computing industry to provide them with these tools, to increase their productivity and their ability to generate profit.

The user is now demanding ever more applications, and the need has been further fuelled by the availability of cheap raw processing power. In a competitive economy there is no choice: either you computerise or you risk losing your position in the marketplace. Whatever estimates for future computer power are used, the productivity of application development must increase by an order of magnitude greater than ten during the next ten years. This cannot happen if computers are programmed using traditional third-generation languages.

As the use of computers spreads, knowledge workers, not DP profession-als, must be able to put them to work. Application development without professional programmers is becoming a necessary trend in computing, if only because there are not enough professional programmers available. Applications will increasingly be created by users, knowledge workers, business consultants and systems analysts. To be productive they need powerful computer languages to build applications. These systems must be built quickly. The main concern and interest of these groups is the business in which they are involved or the application that has to be computerised. It is certainly not the intricacies of coding.

Concentrate on the subject matter

A great photographer concentrates on the subject matter of the picture, not the inner mechanisms of the camera and the properties of the film (although he must have an understanding of these). In the same way a business, systems analyst or knowledge worker should be able to concentrate on the subject matter or problem that concerns him. He must then, be able to put computers to work with powerful application-building tools that can be easily learnt and used with little mental effort. The value of computers in commercial environments is their use in solving problems, not their ability to create coding puzzles.

Spreadsheets start the trend

Perhaps no software product has had such a visible effect on making users employ computers directly than Lotus 123 and other spreadsheet packages. Spreadsheets are decision support tools, enabling users to build up their own models, files and data. They are then ready to manipulate the data, and even perform complex calculations and analyses via formulae. These activities take place on-screen with a captivating and very robust user-friendly interface.

Spreadsheet tools were originally intended for business calculations, but they have found uses among engineers, scientists, and architects as well as in many types of planning and control activities. The user can employ the spreadsheet to forecast future values of data. It can be used to explore the effect of different assumptions and conditions. It can analyse data in many different ways, sort data into columns or rows, and link different spreadsheets together. For many businesses spreadsheets have become the main reason for purchasing personal computers.

Spreadsheets provide an excellent way of reporting complex information. Executives at all levels ought to ask for Lotus-like reports rather than paper listings or terminal access to files. The use of spreadsheets allows managers to explore, manipulate, summarise and plot data as they want.

Spreadsheet reports provide tools for improving communication in business. Different users can have the same representation of complex data, and use the same windows to modify data or try alternative calculations. They can then discuss the modifications. It has become easy to manipulate and analyse data; information can be provided within hours or less. This in turn has led to a greater appreciation of the value of data. Facilities now accepted as standard on PC-based spreadsheets, especially Lotus 123, are the standard by which many users will measure the offerings from the DP department. However, such facilities cannot be provided using traditional DP hardware and software. The use of fourth-generation languages is the only solution.

Fourth-generation languages increase productivity

Fourth-generation languages are used to improve the productivity of those who develop application software as well as that of the end user. Software development tools are now changing as dramatically as the hardware did from the mid-70s to the mid-80s.

These tools, variously known as 'fourth-generation languages', 'high productivity languages', 'non-procedural languages' and 'application generators', offer a way for computer users and DP professionals to provide the applications that have hitherto not been forthcoming.

These tools, available for a number of years, have mostly been used by mainframe DP departments. Now they are available for the user. The reason is twofold. Firstly users have been demanding productivity tools, and understand more about computing so that they are not inhibited by them. Secondly, these tools are now 'user-friendly': someone of average intelligence but with no formal training in programming can use them without the aid of the DP department.

Users will release power of computers

Fourth-generation languages have the potential that will enable the user to release the power of the computer without needing extensive formal training in computer science. Just as spreadsheets were accepted by first-time computer users when personal computers were first introduced into organisations, fourth-generation languages could well shape data processing and mainline computing for the rest of the century.

However, this change will come about in a number of different ways: there is no one sole type of fourth-generation language. They include procedural and non-procedural languages, languages for DP professionals and languages for users, query languages and application generators. Some 4GLs will offer all of these, and some will limit themselves to one or more.

Purists will have their say

Although purists will insist that true 4GLs should exhibit certain features it would be wrong to limit our study only to those. The main thread that links the languages we would group as 4GLs is that they can be used to reduce the development time of application software.

Buyer beware!

The variety and diversity of 4GL products in the marketplace tends to confuse the prospective buyer. He is therefore right to be very cautious. The brochures advertising the products can be misleading. Polishing the good points and glossing over the weak areas. This is also true for the salesmen's presentation and explanation. It is important that those who have to purchase and recommend 4GLs understand the questions to ask, and, more importantly, that they can make sense of the answers given. However, choosing a 4GL is not a once and for all decision. These languages are changing and improving fast, and what was appropriate last year may well have been superseded this year. The relatively stable field of computer languages has suddenly become an area of change, originality and new ideas. In this type of environment it is possible to leap ahead of the pack or fall flat on one's face unless it is understood what is on offer. It is also important to understand the how and why of using them.

Productivity gains imply new management techniques

The dramatic effect of 4GLs on the productivity of data processing staff and departments is legendary and can often be measured in thousands of percentage points. However, this level of productivity is not available to everyone. To achieve the most impressive productivity gains requires a change in both design techniques and project management. It is very important to understand that the design and management techniques needed for the successful implementation of 4GL-based projects are different from those used in a 3GL environment. Some have used 4GLs without basic research, without setting objectives and without planning, leading to cries that the 4GL did not make the productivity gains that were expected.

Many more, however are unaware of the enormous potential of the products. They do not understand how to change their DP structure and thinking to benefit from the potential offered by fourth-generation languages.

DP departments' usefulness questioned

Fourth-generation languages in the hands of users are having a dramatic effect on DP management thinking. Fourth-generation languages are more commonly used in commercial data processing than in scientific and engineering applications. One of the main concerns of the DP professional is that the use of fourth-generation languages raises many management questions. These concern the ways in which the data processing departments should be run. The fact that users have very powerful development tools available to them will mean that the importance of the DP department to an organisation will be questioned.

Decision support systems

The broad field of decision support systems is a prime example of the users' initiative leading the way. Fourth generation languages are more commonly used in decision support systems and management information systems than in routine data processing. If fourth-generation languages are used for systems with high transaction volumes, careful attention must be paid to machine performance. This is because few fourth-generation languages are designed for heavy-duty computing. However, fourth-generation languages can be and are used extensively for creating both prototypes and the final application.

The importance of prototyping

Prototyping is an extremely valuable facility in many areas of data processing and general computing, chiefly because the end user can develop an embryonic system in a very short time and the prototype can be easily adapted and changed. This saves the time needed to write lengthy and detailed specifications that quickly become outdated.

However, individual 4GLs differ greatly in their capabilities, so selecting the right 4GL for the job is very important. There are some horrific stories about attempts to use 4GLs on systems where the applications were not adequate for the task. Some fourth-generation languages will not do the job required: it is necessary to understand what 4GLs are available and what their strengths and weaknesses are. Productivity tools have to be understood and used in the correct situations.

Who is going to give the lead?

Many managers are asking 'Who is going to give the lead?' This question is raised because many managers perceive the DP department as a problem-*creating*, not a problem-*solving* organisation. Whatever the situation, there is a vast backlog of essential applications that have to be developed. It is this situation that has led so many software companies to see the development of 4GLs as a major business opportunity. They are right, but it should also be a major opportunity for the DP departments to regain the initiative. If they do not these tools will be used to reduce the power of the DP departments. Data processing professionals have a choice: either help develop the use of 4GLs in their organisation or suffer a diminution of their standing.

Development of 4GLs marks a watershed

Looking at the history of technology, we can observe certain times when a major break with past methods has occurred. In computing, application methods using third-generation languages have been slowly refined for more than two decades. We have now reached the point when these are inhibiting the most effective use of computers. Fundamentally different methods are needed, and these are now coming into use. Unfortunately many DP organisations are not developing the new methods rapidly enough. When this state of affairs occurs everyone loses out; the company because they are less efficient than they could be and the DP staff, because they are left with skills that are outdated and therefore less valuable. Ask any Fleet Street printer the value of out-of-date skills.

Fourth-generation languages make MIS possible

Management information systems have been created using 4GLs. They provide the capability to extract data from databases and quickly manipulate it in all sorts of different ways. Individuals or departments can create their own view of data, so calculations on it can generate individual reports. They can create summary data and drop down into the detail when necessary. Bulky (and often unintelligible) listings can be replaced with more manageable documentation.

Probably the most important effect of 4GLs is that they have given rise to the possibility of computing by the user as opposed to computing by DP professionals. Historians in the 21st century, looking back at the extraordinary evolution of computing and technology destined to change the entire future of mankind, may comment that a step in that evolution more important than the invention of the transistor was the development of languages that enabled ordinary people to put computers to work. The users, experts at their own discipline or knowledgeable about their own problems, would then know how to develop the computer application that could best help them.

It is interesting to note that the early experience of MIS users capable of building their own applications has highlighted a pent-up demand for using computers that was not met by the traditional DP department.

Need for user-friendly interfaces

Users should be able to build at least some of their own computer facilities. They therefore need languages that are as easy to use as possible – user-friendly languages. Ideally these languages should not require the user to remember mnemonics, formats, sequences, and complex structures. They should be *truly* user-friendly. Eddie Shah, newspaper entrepreneur who uses computers in his operation, commented on one attempt with the remark: '... they [the computers] are as user-friendly as a cornered rat'.

What is a fourth-generation language?

It is often valuable to employ a language designed for a limited set of functions, because such a language can be simpler than a full programming language and carefully targeted to a specific type of application. Lotus 123, for example, gained a vast number of users quickly because it made it easy to structure data and manipulate it in such a way that results and answers to 'what if' questions could be provided in a matter of seconds.

There is likely to be an ongoing controversy about what is and what is not a fourth-generation language. Vendors of 4GLs often refuse to recognise competing products as true fourth-generation languages. Those selling 4GLs that are predominantly non-procedural discount 4GLs with procedural code, and *vice versa*. The debate will go on. The term 'high-productivity language' is perhaps better than fourth-generation language, but if this terminology is used many other products could be grouped under the same heading.

The aim of fourth-generation languages

As James Martin points out in his book *Fourth Generation Languages*, these languages were developed and are being developed to achieve certain objectives, primarily to increase the quality and production of computer applications. Fourth-generation languages were developed as a response to the problems that faced the traditional computer user. They are designed to meet the following objectives:

• To reduce the development cycle of the application building process.

- To make applications easy to modify to reflect the changing nature of business and user requirements.
- To reduce maintenance costs.
- To minimise debugging problems.
- To generate bug-free code from high-level expressions of requirements.
- To make languages user-friendly so that users and knowledge workers can solve their own problems by developing computer systems.

A crucial element of all fourth-generation languages is that they permit applications to be generated with far fewer lines of code than would be needed with COBOL, PL/1, BASIC, or 'C'. This is one of the reasons why fourth-generation languages are known as 'high-productivity' languages.

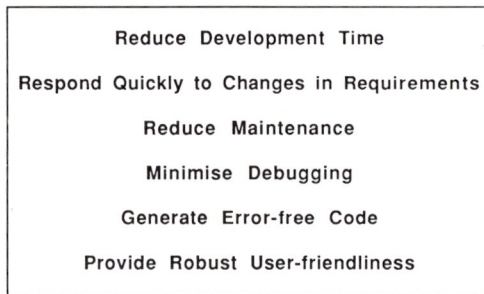

```
┌─────────────────────────────────────────────┐
│                                             │
│         Reduce  Development  Time           │
│                                             │
│  Respond  Quickly to Changes in Requirements│
│                                             │
│           Reduce  Maintenance               │
│                                             │
│            Minimise  Debugging              │
│                                             │
│          Generate  Error-free  Code         │
│                                             │
│       Provide  Robust  User-friendliness    │
│                                             │
└─────────────────────────────────────────────┘
```

Fig. 3.1 The aims of a 4GL.

Many fourth-generation languages that run under DOS and UNIX are closely linked to a database and its data dictionary. The dictionary has in some cases evolved into a facility that can represent more than the data. It may contain screen formats, report formats, dialogue structures, associations between data, validity checks, security controls, clearance to read or modify data, calculations that are used to create derived fields, permissible ranges, and logical relationships among data values. The extension of the dictionary that contains business rules and logic is sometimes referred to as an encyclopaedia.

A major concern in the assessment or purchase of a fourth-generation language is the infrastructure needed to support it, which includes databases, libraries, dictionaries and encyclopaedias.

Principles of fourth-generation languages

Some basic principles of fourth-generation languages are as follows:

(1) **The principle of minimum work.** The aim is to put computers to work with the minimum of effort.

(2) **The principle of minimum skill.** The aim is to put computers to work as easily as possible, without the need for users to undergo long and complex training. This is to enable a larger cross-section of the public to use computers in their daily work.

(3) **The principle of minimum complexity.** The aim is to avoid alien syntax and mnemonics. Language construction should be clear and succinct, and as close to English as possible.

(4) **The principle of minimum time.** The aim is to make it possible to use computers without waiting a long time for application development.

(5) **The principle of minimum error.** The aim is to devise techniques that reduce the probability of human error, and if possible to catch those errors that do occur automatically.

(6) **The principle of minimum maintenance.** The aim is to ensure that the data structure allows for easy modification to accommodate changing needs.

(7) **The principle of maximum results.** The aim is to be able to develop computer applications that are as powerful, useful and valuable as possible. This should be achieved in a productive and efficient manner.

If we use these criteria as a method of assessing what is and what is not a fourth-generation language, we will be closer to using computers to tackle many outstanding business problems. This should make things easier and simpler than they would otherwise have been. 4GLs embody the key to success for most ventures – KISS (Keep It Simple, Stupid!).

Application generators and traditional languages

Application generators can be distinguished from traditional languages by the level of the facilities that they present to the application developer. For example, consider the code required to accept input into a field on a form – in a traditonal language the programmer would have to write statements to write code for the display of the form, to move the cursor to the desired location on the screen, accept input characters one at a time, check for terminators and for the end of field, and so on. This simple operation would take many lines of code. In a typical 4GL, this same application could be accomplished within a few lines of code. Other sophisticated built-in functions supported by many application generators include menu and report generation, WYSIWYG (What You See Is What You Get) form editors, and easy data formatting controls.

Obviously, not all operations lend themselves to built-in functions. For example, complex arithmetic computations are probably done more efficiently using current programming languages. It is this factor which ensures that most application generators include at least some standard programming language features, such as assignment, branch, loop and conditional statements. These capabilities, and more advanced ones, make these products potentially very powerful tools for application development.

End-user tools and support systems

Application generators, however, are only one subset of the 4GL spectrum. Many other products tend to be designed to address a single (if sometimes large) problem area. They are geared towards the average computer user. Such products are often labelled *end-user productivity tools*, or sometimes even *decision support systems*. End-user tools, by their very nature, try to avoid most traditional programming features. Instead, they concentrate on visual and simple command-driven interfaces.

Fourth-generation languages fall into two wide categories

Most products marketed as 4GLs fall into one of these two large categories. Even the distinction between the two, however, can fast become hazy as one gets closer into these products. Many people have made careers from teaching integrated packages, and writing templates and macros for them. A good Lotus 123 macro writer is necesarily a programmer working in that language. Additionally, the more professional tools now offer powerful capabilities for untrained users. For example, many popular database systems offer tools that allow users to build forms and reports and to query files without ever coming near a programming language.

Both product groups, of course, would like to have universal appeal. Sadly, however, most industry observers seem to agree that the dream of a single product that is powerful enough to build a complete accounting package, and yet simple enough to allow an untrained user to feel comfortable, has posed a problem which 4GLs continue to try to solve. Many packages, of course, fall somewhere between a total development system and the simple program that can be built in an hour. In those cases application programmers, whether programming professionals or novice users, must examine the wide array of available tools to see which one can solve their problem.

Basic goal is to increase productivity

All of these tools achieve, to a greater or lesser degree, their basic goal of making users more productive than they would be if traditional programming languages were used. However, applications built with such tools carry an additional cost. They often require significantly greater computer resources than if they were written in traditional programming languages. However, this is less important now that the cost of processing power is steadily going down.

When faced with an application need for which they cannot buy a ready-made solution, more and more users are turning to fourth-generation languages. Although reluctant to learn a traditional programming language, many of them nevertheless become quite expert in a 4GL. Professional application developers are also turning to 4GLs in order to develop better products more quickly than was possible before.

The numbers of users and the variety of their application needs, together with the increasing power of computers, all point to an explosive growth in fourth generation languages.

Dividing user computing

It is important to divide user computing into that which is purely personal and that which is shared. In truly personal computing the user develops his own tools or filing system for his own purposes. Nobody else uses them, except, perhaps, close associates. There is no need to develop documentation for other users or to conform to the rules of data administration or DP standards. This is the province of personal computing. The shared computer relates to an environment in which applications are used by many people, and may be modified or maintained by others. Data used here may be created elsewhere. In some corporations shared applications are created by users, and have proved to be extremely valuable. Shared computing needs careful attention to documentation, user ability, maintenance, testing and integral controls as well as data administration control. The software selected should facilitate these controls.

Some 4GLs are largely self-documenting and encourage the application developer to add comments and 'help displays'. The majority of 4GLs are designed to work in conjunction with a database management system employing data dictionaries with data administration. Some employ an encyclopaedia which provides important controls.

Some 4GLs are good for maintenance and some are not. If a language is good for maintenance, it is possible to read somebody else's code and understand it readily so that it is easy to modify. When it is modified, all the consequential changes that ought to be made as a result of the modification should be clear, and where possible will be made automatically.

The market for fourth-generation languages for UNIX and DOS

The market for PC- and UNIX-based fourth-generation languages is becoming increasingly developed. Nearly every database management system sports a set of tools which are sold as a 4GL. The large diversity among these products can be quite confusing. However, this product growth is not happening in a vacuum. The growing number and acceptance of 4GLs indicates both a real consumer need and the fact that personal computers today are able to meet their extensive resource requirements. To understand 4GLs today it helps to examine the reasons behind the growth in customer demand. Some basic guidance for classifying the many packages sold as 4GLs will also be helpful, and this is provided in a later chapter. It will help users to assess the benefit and value of 4GLs and determine where they may be used as an appropriate application development tool.

Chapter Four
The DOS and UNIX Marketplace

In order to appreciate the significance of the DOS and UNIX marketplace it is essential to understand what an operating system is and how it interacts between programs and devices.

What is an operating system?

The software component of a computer system is becoming more and more complex. It is useful to see it in terms of a layered shell. The different layers of the shell represent the different layers of software, which all need to interact with each other.

The outermost layer of the shell is the *user interface* the way the system interacts with the user as he sits at the keyboard. The user will normally be running an application program. In some cases, particularly in some of the fourth-generation languages, this is part of the application program. In other cases it comes within the operating system. In an effort to hide the operating system from the user, there is a welcome trend for software products such as Microsoft's *Windows*, which is a general purpose user interface, enabling software and operating system services to be used in a standard format based on simple graphics. This avoids the need to learn new ways of doing the same thing.

The application program is the next layer

The next layer down is the application program – in other words the invoicing program, or the application that has been developed using the fourth-generation language, or whatever piece of software the machine is being used for.

The layer below the application program is in many cases a *database management system*; this is the case with many powerful fourth-generation languages. The database management system consists of special software that looks after the files of data, creating indexes so that it is possible to get at a particular record easily, keeping track of changes that have been made so that there is a record of what has happened, and so on.

The operating system itself

Finally we come to the *operating system* itself. This is the software which looks after the detailed handling of the various devices that make up the computer, interpreting the keys that are pressed, deciding what character to display on the screen, handling errors and interrupts, etc. In essence it manages the resources of the computer, i.e. storage, back-up units, display, and communication with peripheral devices.

Operating systems are machine managers

Much of the operating system will be concerned with managing the disk and the files stored on it, keeping track of where each file starts and ends, and allowing the user to copy, rename, add, and delete files. Another part deals with programs, finding each program when it is wanted for use and setting it running, taking over when the program has finished, and stepping in if the program needs to use an input or output device.

Often the operating system itself is in layers – for instance, an upper level will actually instruct the disk head to move so many steps in towards the centre to find the data in question. The lower-level parts of an operating system – the kernel and the specialised device drivers – must nearly always be custom-written for different hardware. The upper levels, on the other hand, can be generalised, so that the same operating system can be implemented on different machines.

The benefit of the layered shell approach is that each level of software has a clearly-defined range of functions and can therefore be written more easily. Moreover, the application program does not need to concern itself with details of how the hardware works, as the operating system will handle it. The program's interface with the hardware is achieved indirectly via system function calls, supplied as part of the operating system and available to the application developer.

Types of operating system

The type of operating system required depends very much on the size and complexity of the computer. DOS, for instance, is specifically designed for a small computer like the PC, and one which has rather limited objectives – in particular it is a *single-stream* operating system.

Single-stream operating systems can only have one program or job running at a time. While the job is running, the operating system functions passively, responding to specific calls for hardware resources, but otherwise has little to do. At the end of a program the scheduling function of the operating system is awakened and takes action to load the next process, perhaps awaiting a command from the operator. Obviously there must be a standard way for it to be given such commands: in fact this is done by means of a special language, which is understood by a part of the operating system called the *command interpreter*.

The use of the term 'single-stream' implies that there are such things as *multiple-stream* operating systems, and indeed there are, most of them initially designed for much larger machines than the PC. They allow a number of programs or users to access the computer simultaneously. In this case there is much more for the operating system to do; it must take an active role all the time, sharing the machine and its various resources between competing tasks. The new generation of PCs based on the Intel 386 have the necessary power to support multiple-stream operating systems.

Machine independence

At one time every brand of computer had its own operating system. Today, however, the trend is towards machine-independent' operating systems that can run differing hardware. This is not such a strange idea; after all, one of the functions of any operating system is to hide the details of the hardware from the user or the application programmer so that he can concentrate on the problem at hand, without needing to know the precise characteristics of different devices. The logical extension of this principle is an 'industry standard' operating system, which can allow the user to run the same programs on a number of different types of computer, even from different manufacturers.

MS-DOS and PC-DOS and the history of single stream operating systems

The operating system used by the IBM PC has been copied by many other manufacturers, and is now the most widely used single-user operating system. It is interesting to note the history of the DOS operating system.

Before 16-bit micros came into general use, Digital Research pioneered the idea of a machine-independent operating system called CP/M (Control

Program for Microcomputers). It became the industry standard operating system for 8-bit machines – or at least, for those based on the Z80 and 8080 microprocessor. They were developing a 16-bit version (CP/M-86) at the time that IBM was looking for an operating system for their new Personal Computer. Digital Research's market dominance made them the obvious choice. Suprisingly, IBM gave the commission to Microsoft, who were mainly known as a supplier not of operating systems, but of programming languages.

Microsoft enter the arena and win

Microsoft produced an operating system very similar to CP/M-86 for IBM. It was officially called IBM Personal Computer DOS, and unofficially PC-DOS. A version was also produced for non-IBM machines, called MS-DOS. Today, MS-DOS and PC-DOS are virtually identical, although differences arise between the IBM PC and other MS-DOS machines because of the underlying ROM BIOS, which is copyright to IBM and can not be copied in other machines.

There have been three major versions of MS-DOS up to now. MS-DOS 1.0 was a very simple operating system, similar in operation and functionality to CP/M. MS-DOS 2.2 added a number of features copied from UNIX, such as subdirectories and pathnames, redirection of input and output, and background print spooling. MS-DOS 3.1 gives basic facilities for networking several PCs together, and allows you to use a 'RAM disk'. Finally MS-DOS 3.2 adds several useful items, including advanced commands for copying and replacing files in various subdirectories, and also better safeguards against the possibility of deleting information on the hard disk storage unit.

Importance of industry standard operating systems

The development of DOS as the 'de facto' standard has brought about numerous advantages for the user, and very few for the traditional computer manufacturers. IBM's disappointing profit figures during '85, '86 and '87 have in part been due to the way in which the personal computer market slipped from their grasp. Many new entrants came into the market with machines that were faster, cheaper and equipped with more functions. All these machines used the same operating system and the same size disk. This meant that users could upgrade their machines, swop data on disks, use the same application software, and generally work in a stable environment irrespective of the machine they used – IBM, Compaq, Zenith, Olivetti, Tandy, Amstrad and the many PC clones from the Far East were all virtually data interchangeable.

The user was spared the trauma of learning different ways of doing the same thing and could concentrate on using the machine to improve the effiency of whatever tasks he had to undertake. The user's importance to an organisation is the way in which he uses the power of the computer to increase the productivity of the company. In order to do this easily the machine has to be standard, the operating systems have to be standard, the application software has to be standard, and the way in which the machine is operated has to be standard – the one thing the user does not want is for computer manufacturers to make their machine non-standard by adding bits and pieces to the operating system or the machine itself. Unfortunately, this is what many traditional computer manufacturers wish to do. The question to be answered is 'Who will win; the customer and consumer or the manufacturer and supplier?' DP managers and users should make up their minds where their loyalties lie and fight their corner.

Information as a resource has to be protected

The need for a standard operating system is even more urgent for multi-user computers. It is not only necessary to have standard commands, application software and peripherals – but it is vital that the data stored is standardised and protected. If, as has been stated by many experts, data and information is a valuable resource that any organisation can group with capital, machinery and labour, then it should surely be protected just as carefully.

If non-standard or proprietary operating systems are used to develop organisational databases and systems, the data or information contained on these systems is 'trapped', or at least very closely linked to a particular computer manufacturer. This situation has been allowed to happen for a number of reasons: historic reasons, senior management's lack of under-standing of computing, DP managers' lack of understanding of the commercial realities, and the awesome power of some computer companies.

If it works, does it matter?

There are those who say that if the system works and is supported by a large and profitable company it does not matter what operating system is used – as long as it is supported. However, the systems that are developed and the data that is stored are resources belonging to the organisation in the same way as capital, machines and manpower. When a proprietary operating system is used the data is 'stamped' or 'marked' in such a way that it is impossible, or extremely difficult, to use on another system. This is an untenable situation.

Treat information like capital

Can anyone imagine a board of directors or a company chairman limiting their other resources in the same way? If we look at capital, would they use money or capital from only one source, without being able to exchange the capital or use capital from other markets? Of course not. The free market ethos is that resources should be free to find their own level. Money and capital should be able to flow unfettered to and from those markets that will

$$\boxed{\text{Information}} = \boxed{£\ £\ £}$$

Fig. 4.1   Information is capital.

be able to utilise it to the full. It should not be 'marked' in such a way that it can only be used in clearly defined areas. If this were the case the situation would be inefficient and alarming. The same is true for machinery, labour and information. So why restrict the use of the company's life-blood – its data or information? There is a need for a standard multi-user operating system to protect companies' information systems. There are many other aspects to this argument that have been spelt out in our other books. However, the view put forward here is beginning to be understood, and as a result a battle to supply (and control) the industry standard multi-user operating system has already begun.

The battle for the multi-user PC

Both MS-DOS and PC-DOS are single-user operating systems, and the PC is essentially a single-user machine. Past attempts to make PCs multi-user via XENIX, BOS, or Concurrent DOS, let alone MP/M, were always doomed to failure for performance reasons. The IBM PC is slow enough to be irksome at times as a single-user machine; as a multi-user computer it is intolerable. What the PC and DOS did highlight is the need to have an 'industry standard' multi-user operating system. For many reasons this task is likely to fall to the UNIX operating system.

The development of a game starts UNIX

In 1969 Ken Thompson, working at Bell Laboratories, the research arm of

AT&T, started the development of a 'space travel' game. The machine used was a General Electric 645 mainframe. However, the complexity of the mainframe and its unsuitability for single user interaction led him to develop the program on a DEC PDP-7, one of the earliest minicomputers. The PDP lacked the tools that a software developer can expect today. Ken's natural inclination was to write a suitable operating system. He did, and added an assembler and utilities to support development work. UNIX was born.

UNIX, the castrated operating system

A number of features from existing operating systems of the time found their way into UNIX, especially from the Multics operating system, which was a joint development between AT&T and General Electric. AT&T withdrew from the development of Multics before work on UNIX began. One reason given for the name UNIX is that it is a 'castrated' version of Multics!

The UNIX operating system started out on small minicomputers, but today it is available on all sizes of computer from personal computers up to the largest 'super-computer'. UNIX was widely issued to universities, and has only recently been adopted for business use.

The three phases of UNIX

In the first phase, UNIX was bought on its merits as a flexible and powerful development environment for building systems. It was loved by programmers since it provided those very tools that reduced the time-consuming and repetitive tasks associated with system development. It was very expensive (except to educational establishments) and AT&T provided no support.

In the second phase, UNIX was developed by third parties, who saw the opportunity to enter the computer manufacturing industry by supplying UNIX-based systems, saving the research and development costs that would have been incurred if they had decided to develop their own operating system. These machines were sold under a variety of names. Organisations began to buy systems based on UNIX because it offered a common standard which they could use on many types of hardware.

In the third phase AT&T have taken the initiative. They have been split up and deregulated by the US authorities, and are now willing and able to support UNIX worldwide. Their new System V version is beginning to draw the various versions together, offering the best of each in a unified package.

The history of UNIX has been a chequered one, and would undoubtedly have been very different had IBM invented it. Having brought UNIX into the world, AT&T abandoned its parental rights so soon that others had a decisive hand in its upbringing. As the child approaches maturity, its parent is trying to regain control by defining a standard UNIX in the form of System V.

UNIX versions and variants

It is possible to purchase the source code to UNIX from AT&T via a licence agreement. Many companies did so and produced different versions of UNIX, all with different names, which has confused the issue. IBMs AIX, DECs ULTRIX and Microsoft's XENIX are three such versions. However, it is important to make it clear that AIX, ULTRIX, XENIX and many others, are 'real UNIX' – in other words they are derived from original source code issued by AT&T, and every time you buy a copy of AIX, ULTRIX or XENIX part of the purchase price ends up with AT&T as a licence fee.

Companies also went independent and produced UNIX-like operating systems from scratch, without buying a source licence. These have included such names as Cromix, Coherent, and UNOS. It is unlikely that there will be a future for these 'look-alikes'.

Reasons for banking on UNIX

There are a number of pointers suggesting that UNIX may develop into the de facto standard for a multi-user operating system. First, there are a large number of start-up computer companies who see UNIX as a method by which they can enter the multi-user market with a certain amount of credibility. Second, IBM, DEC and the others who have proprietary operating systems support UNIX, if only because they are afraid they will miss out if they do not. Third, AT&T – with their power and financial clout – are backing UNIX to the hilt and ensuring that there is one standard UNIX.

The acceptance of UNIX as the standard multi-user operating system still has some way to go, but there are positive signals that it could well achieve this goal:

- The US government (especially the Department of Defense) and agencies are increasingly stipulating UNIX as the operating system for all the computers they purchase for office automation systems, and they purchase more computers than anyone else.
- General Motors and other large US corporations have begun to standardise on UNIX for the thousands of small computers they use.
- Companies new to computing have decided to become supplierindependent by taking the UNIX route.

Advantages of UNIX

The advantage of UNIX is that it is supported by the US Department of Defense and other major user organisations. AT&T are spending vast sums of money developing UNIX, and this development is available to all manufacturers that offer UNIX as their main operating system. For the user, a major plus is the portability (within limits). The user is not locked to any computer manufacturer. Another advantage is that the fourth generation languages available under UNIX are among the most innovative and powerful in the industry.

POSIX, the portable operating system

POSIX, the portable operating system environment, is an interface standard that is being developed by the IEEE Computer Society. Its aim is to provide a truly vendor-independent portable operating system based on UNIX, but distinguished from AT&T's UNIX trademark. The major computer manufacturers have declared support for the POSIX standard. Small companies will be able to spread their applications across a wider range of hardware when the standard is fully established, and it offers the key for the migration of applications into the UNIX environment.

The major problem in accepting POSIX as the standard for a portable operating system is in resolving the small number of interface differences between AT&T's UNIX System V Release 3.0 and POSIX. Once these are solved and POSIX becomes the standard then AT&T will lose direct control over the future form of UNIX and the world will enter an era of true vendor-independent computing.

Disadvantages of UNIX

There are a number of disadvantages that prevent some purists even considering the UNIX route. Although they have a number of valid points it should be remembered that DOS is not the ideal operating system, by any manner of means, but it became the de facto standard.

- UNIX has a high overhead. Some estimate that it is at least 3 times as high as DEC's VMS, which is not an optimal system.
- The flexibility provided by UNIX can lead to over-tooling if the developers are not controlled. The use of UNIX can therefore lead to unstructured and inefficient systems.
- Priority-driven is not a native UNIX characteristic. The system is time-

slicing, and as such is not the ideal answer for some commercial applications.
- UNIX was not developed as a commercial offering, and the way in which it is presented demonstrates this fact.
- UNIX is still developing, and as yet system functions have not been optimised to guarantee predictable response times.

Differences between DOS and UNIX

DOS – particularly version 2.0 and later versions – appears very similar to UNIX, and does in fact incorporate a number of ideas borrowed from UNIX. However, a closer look reveals some major differences. For instance, both systems have subdirectories and both have pipes, but the way these are implemented is very different.

The key difference is that DOS is single-tasking and single-user, whereas UNIX is multi-tasking and multi-user. It is because of the multi-user aspect that UNIX files and directories are assigned to individual owners, and thus help to provide the security features that multi-user systems need. Additionally, knowledge workers need to use windows to carry out a number of different tasks at the same time, so the ability to multi-task will be crucial.

UNIX, DOS and 4GLs

There are many indications that the combination of industry-standard operating systems (DOS and UNIX) and fourth-generation languages is a very exciting one. The stability of the UNIX marketplace and the clear indication that it will emerge as the de facto industry standard multi-user operating system has encouraged many of the best minds to overcome some of UNIXs deficiences and develop application software for this market. The result is that the standard of application and productivity software available in the UNIX marketplace is superior to that available in any other multi-user market.

Chapter Five
Databases and their Management

The study and understanding of databases within a fourth-generation environment is important. This is because the majority of the current crop of 4GLs in the marketplace are linked to an underlying database management system. The succesful management of databases requires certain skills that have to be understood.

Data is increasingly regarded as the basic resource needed to operate a corporation. As with other basic resources, the professional management of data is a primary prerequisite. The effective use of data for production control, marketing, accounting, planning and other business functions will become so significant that it will have an effect on the growth and survival of companies in the competitive marketplace.

These developments have meant that databases and their management have become one of the most important aspects of computing. In the past most information was recorded using pen and ink, and later on the typewriter. Now companies require more sophisticated methods. But first, what is data and what is information?

What is information?

Information is now a science, and has the grand title 'information theory'. A modest definition of information is 'useful data'. The difference between *data*, or inert facts, and *information*, or facts that satisfy a requirement, is not in the data itself; it is in the question that is asked.

An example illustrating the difference between data and information is the telephone directory. It contains millions of data items in the form of names, addresses and telephone numbers. This inert data does not become information until you ask a question (for example 'What is the telephone number of such-and-such a company?'). In providing the answer to the question, the inert data becomes information. But look what happens if you have a telephone number and want to find out the name and address it belongs to. The data is certainly contained in the telephone directory; you can

Question: What is the telephone number for Digitus Ltd.?

Telephone Directory

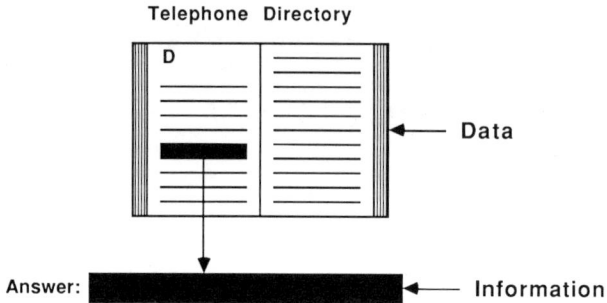

Fig. 5.1 Data and information.

certainly ask the question; but it is almost impossible to obtain the information, because of the way in which the data is arranged.

This highlights a major problem in many businesses: a lot of data is stored in filing cabinets under the misapprehension that it is information. In reality the data is often filed in such a way that it is impossible to obtain answers to the questions asked. It is inert or useless data. One of the benefits of today's computer systems, if they are properly organised, is that databases can be constructed to allow the data to be accessed in many *different* ways and turned into valuable information.

Batch processing was not ideal

The first type of computerised database was based on *batch processing*. Batch processing, with data rigidly divided into separate files for each application, was not the ideal way to operate in a dynamic commercial environment. It would have been much more convenient for management to have all the information about their organisation up-to-date and at their fingertips. However, because of the nature of data processing techniques management was living with a compromise. Today's compromise has been in existence for so long that it has become an accepted method of operation, and little thought has been given to its effectiveness.

Using a database is like having a superbly fast and brilliant clerk who keeps data for many applications. He organises books so that a minimum of writing is necessary and so that he can search the books quickly to answer any query that may come along. Unlike his pedestrian predecessor, who could write or read items only in one ledger, he rushes from one set of data to another

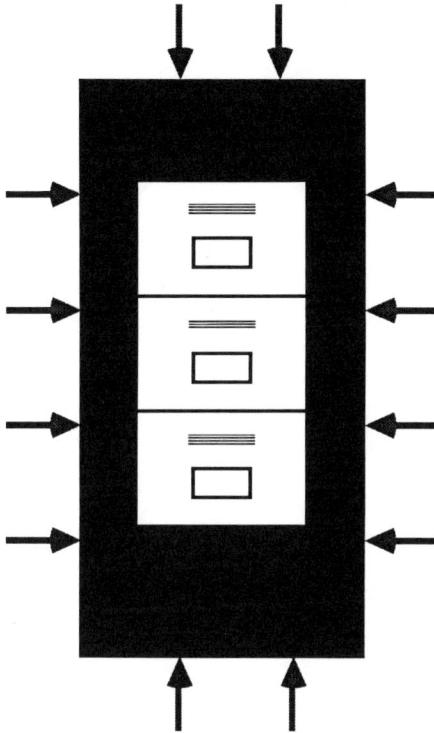

Fig. 5.2 Data in filing cabinets is not information.

collating separate items to respond to a wide variety of requests for information. He is a godsend to management.

Information needs span departments

Executives often need information which spans departments or traditional boundaries in the corporation, such as engineering, accounting, personnel, production, and marketing functions. They require information on the personnel implications of marketing decisions, or the impact on production of new distribution strategies, or the labour costs associated with higher sales. The wages department may have its own batch processing operation, and can be of little value in answering some questions. With the database approach, however, the super clerk rushes from one department to another searching for and collating data. The structure of the data that is stored is agreed at one central point so that interdepartmental use is possible.

Value of data depends on its use

The value of data depends on the use to which it is put. Today, data should be an important element in the decision-making process for most organisations. This data is often in a machine-readable form that is not available to the decision makers when they need it. Furthermore, the cost of producing new computer programs and modifying old ones is often extraordinarily high because the data is not in the right format. To make data as useful as possible, and to control system development costs, appropriate design of data systems is necessary.

Decision makers can have far better information than they had before computers, and they can have it just when they need it. However, the task of building up an information source is exceedingly complex, and many managers have underestimated the difficulties involved.

Data, both for routine operations such as invoice and payroll and for supportive decision making (whether computerised or not) resides in computer storage units. The corporation will have various different collections of data for different purposes and different locations. They may be linked by communication lines to the machine, or by people who employ them. They can differ widely in their structure. The intention of a database is to allow the same collection of data to serve as many applications as is useful.

Hence the database is often conceived of as a repository of the information needed for running certain functions of e.g. a corporation, a factory, a university, or a department store. A database permits not only the retrieval of data but also the continuous *modification* of data needed for the control of operations. It may be possible to search the database to obtain answers to queries, or information for planning purposes. The collection of data may serve several departments, often cutting across political boundaries.

The much publicised 'dream database' allows an organisation to keep all this information in a large reservoir, in which a diversity of data users can 'go fishing'. Such a database would be highly complex; as a rule the dream is far from being achieved in reality. It will remain a worthy goal of data processing well into the 21st century. The user of complex data has to be educated stage by stage. In reality most databases today serve a varied but limited set of applications. Many different databases are used for different purposes. Eventually the databases for separate related functions may become combined where this integration can increase the efficiency or usefulness of the overall system. A major task of corporations over the next few years is deciding what databases they need, where they are best located, what data should be stored in them and how they should be organised. Large, progressive organisations already store a vast amount of data on their computer storage units, and the volume of data being stored will increase dramatically. The *way* that this data is stored will fundamentally affect its usefulness. This is a growth area, and one where 4GLs linked to databases will be of great help. However, the task has to be managed.

Database administrator

A new job title, *database administrator*, has been created for the person who presides over the task of developing a database. The database administrator is custodian of the data. He controls its overall structure and maintenance. It is a very important job that combines a heady mixture of technology and organisational politics.

Being custodian of the data is quite separate from being the owner. The bank manager is the custodian of what the bank holds but he is not the owner. The department or the individual may own the data. The database administrator is responsible for keeping and controlling the data. The data may be used by any person given authority to do so. Further, controlling the data does not imply that the database administrator knows the contents of records. He knows that the payroll record contains a salary data field but he does not know the value recorded in that field: indeed, he is specifically locked out of that data item so that he cannot read it.

The database administrator maintains the overall view of the data in his domain. He encourages standardisation of data items and determines what data structures and layout will be best for the data user as a whole. He attempts to referee the feuds that develop between departments or divisions about the nature of the data. If an application programmer wants to create a new type of record, modify an existing record by including new data items, or expand the size of the data item, he must apply to the database administrator for permission.

The database administrator will make suitable arrangements to modify the data structure to whatever extent he thinks best for the system as a whole. An applications programmer or a systems analyst working on one application is not permitted to change the overall data structure: only the database administrator or his staff, who have a global viewpoint, can be familiar with the overall economics of the data.

There are a variety of other functions associated with the keeper of the corporation's data. We will discuss those functions more fully later on.

A complete understanding of a database – its organisation, its economics, its design criteria and the requirements of its many users – may be too much for one man.

High level data administration

A large corporation has many databases, a number of data processing centres and often a number of database administrators. It is increasingly becoming recognised that top management involvement is needed in the planning of the overall information resource of the organisation. One individual in the top ranks of the organisation should be responsible for that organisation's data – both computerised and non-computerised. This individual is often known as the *Information Director*.

Three levels of management

When thinking about management information it is important to distinguish between the needs of different levels of management. Three levels of activity are generally distinguished in an organisation. Level one operations can be almost completely automated. Level two operations can be partly automated but need management involvement. Level three operations require intelligent human thinking with assistance from computers.

Level One: Routine operations and reflex actions
- Recording of customer orders
- Breakdown of parts and sub-assemblies
- Shop floor data collection
- Preparation of work tickets
- Maintaining inventory records
- Reordering parts and materials
- Production of purchase orders
- Goods receiving
- Payment of supplies
- Accounts receivable and payable
- Goods shipping
- Invoicing
- General Ledger
- Cost Accounting
- Costing
- Payroll
- Quality control

Level Two: Well-defined management operations
- Setting working budgets
- Planning working capital
- Determining prices

- Choosing suppliers
- Sales management
- Short-term forecasting
- Production scheduling
- Shop floor monitoring
- Maintenance management
- Routine personnel administration
- Formulating rules for transport operations

Level Three: Strategic planning and creative decision-making
- Determination of markets
- Long-range forecasting
- Directing research
- Choosing new products
- Setting financial policies
- Setting personal policies

Top management questions

Most of the questions that top management ask relate to Level Three and cannot be answered directly by today's computer systems. Top management does not tend to ask questions that can be answered by examining and correlating data items (e.g. 'What percentage of sales quota did branches X, Y, and Z make in November?'). They are more likely to ask such questions as 'Why are sales down?' or 'What changes could be made to the sales teams' compensation plan for next year?'

Chapter Six
The Information Centre and Fourth-Generation Languages

To obtain the maximum benefit from fourth generation languages it is necessary to develop an environment in which they can flourish. This means understanding the attributes and characteristics both of fourth-generation languages and of the users who are going to employ these development tools. If the languages are to be used by non-computing end users then the provision of an information centre can be very beneficial.

However, before a system can be developed using fourth-generation languages the language has to be selected. Due to the proliferation of products on offer this can be a very daunting task, especially in the DOS and UNIX environment. Support and guidance when making these types of decision can be provided by the information centre.

The rapid rise of the information centre

A 1986 US survey by the American Management Association found that 40% of all US businesses using computers – and 80% of billion dollar corporations – have an established and growing information centre. Among corporations, 79% of the information centres had been set up between 1983 and the present. Information centres in companies with an annual turnover between $50 million and $500 million have been set up since 1985.

The survey found that the average corporate information centre has 4.5 staff and serves the users of 47 stand-alone PCs, four PCs linked to either a minicomputer or mainframe, and 40 dumb terminals. Projections for the next year show that these figures will be 66 stand-alone PCs, 18 PCs linked by a network or to a larger machine, and 48 dumb terminals.

Information centres were found to be playing a major role in the evaluation of hardware and software, as well as approving the purchase. Information centres were originally formed by DP departments to serve as mediators between themselves and the growing number of users. A third of information centres were found to have their own budget, separate from the DP department. However, the remainder served the DP manager and user. The most interesting fact highlighted by the report was that information centre managers find themselves approaching DP managers with ever-increasing budgets for approval, yet at the same time making further inroads into territory that was once the province of the DP department. These conflicts will not remain a problem in the future if all information centres are autonomous and ultimately answerable to the user.

The need for management

When end users, especially first time end users, start to create applications for themselves, they need a lot of training, handholding, encouragement and comforting. There is a learning curve for all products and during this learning period the trainee requires sympathetic help and encouragement. Too often non-DP users have given up in frustration because they were not helped appropriately or did not have access to the data and tools most useful to them. It is the role of DP management to ensure that this support is available in some form or other. In general, end user computing needs to be managed. Without help, training and controls, all kinds of problems can develop, and more often than not the DP department will be asked to clear up the mess. It is therefore in the best interest of all DP departments to provide the support necessary.

The information centre

There are many methods of providing support, but the information centre is a very useful management vehicle for end-user computing. A commercial organisation requires an information centre for the following reasons:

(1) To support the user throughout the start-up period.
(2) To ensure that users have access to data and tools most appropriate to them and their needs.
(3) To help users develop applications as efficiently as possible.
(4) To help avoid the numerous types of mistake that users can make and will make if not guided.
(5) To encourage the concept of end-user computing in order that it may reach its full potential.
(6) To ensure that the systems developed can be linked and shared by other systems within that organisation, so that data entered or maintained by the user is seen as a *corporate* resource and not an isolated personal electronic filing cabinet. Information must be shared and used, not hoarded away.

(7) To keep some measure of control over the accuracy of data used in the systems.
(8) To provide a facility that enables end-users to share systems and modules rather than allowing numerous people to develop the same system.
(9) To avoid integrity problems caused by repeated updating of data.
(10) To help ensure that systems are built with the necessary audit and security features when necessary.
(11) To ensure the relevant requirements of the Data Protection Act are understood and followed.

The information centre's concept

The rationale of the information centre is to support a natural division of labour among the DP staff. Each group should provide the services it is best equipped to supply. The end users usually know what information and decision support they need to do their job. They invariably need results quickly. The DP support group should know how these results can be obtained. The two groups should work together in a close partnership, balancing the resources for the maximum productivity of the organisation.

Walls, not bridges, tend to be built

To understand the importance of information centres, examine the traditional way in which systems are developed. The formal development life-cycle requires written specifications to be created. Although this takes a lot of time it is rarely adequate. This is because the specification must be frozen at the start of the design phase. Unfortunately it is often frozen when the ideas about what the system ought to do are still fluid. The programmer is more often

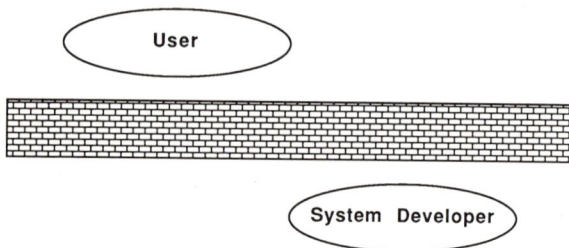

Fig. 6.1 Walls not bridges are built between users and developers.

than not kept away from the end user. The user often does not know what he wants until he sees it on a terminal and uses it, and this is becoming increasingly true as we move towards more immediate decision support applications and systems. The traditional techniques for application development tend to build a wall between the application user and the application creator.

Standard applications (e.g. payroll, invoicing) have been developed and are readily available, usually in a packaged form. Now is the time to tackle other systems that the users want. Every organisation is faced with the need for complex and valuable applications such as decision support, operations control, and financial planning systems. These applications require a rapid rate of adjustment when users begin to change their methods of working.

Valued advice is always advisable

Even if the user is going to develop the system, using 4GLs on a computer under DOS or UNIX, it is wise to seek the advice of a computer specialist who has been involved with system development using 4GLs. However, the naive user has to be considered when a 4GL is used in the decision support or operational environment.

The 4GL specialist should have a clear picture

The 4GL specialist should have a clear picture of the product best suited to the users' needs, but the issue is by no means black and white. Since products claim to meet all needs that could be envisaged, whether on a personal computer or in a mainframe environment, it is important to talk to end users in depth and discuss systems that have been developed. The DP manager cannot assess the real strengths of various products by reading a directory of computer software or manufacturers' literature.

These documents are not technically deficient, but many products can answer 'yes' to a check list of questions such as 'Is the product based on a relational database?'. There is a world of potential difference between a product which provides query facilities across its flat file structure and one which has the full power of the relational calculus behind its operation. It is important to understand both the question and the answer.

There are a number of methods of making an assessment, but one of the more sensible approaches is to carry out trials. First the type of 4GL has to be selected. After selecting the type most appropriate to the needs of the organisation, it is necessary to identify the functional requirements, study the success and stability of the product, contact its supplier and establish the cost, and attend the vendors' 'demos' in order to shortlist three products, at most, for trial.

The trial

If the department checks the key requirements of the product when benchmark testing, it is likely to achieve the golden '80/20' rule: getting 80% of the information one might gather from a fully comprehensive investigation with 20% of the effort. The decision might be made with less than 100% of the information, but at least it will be made within a sensible timescale and with the most important elements of information.

It can also be helpful to make full use of independent user groups to contact organisations with practical experience of the various offerings. It is always worth talking to live users about the product and the way that they have used it. It is from these sources that you are most likely to determine the truth about the product's strengths and weaknesses.

If there are any critical functional requirements which may be important to your organisation they have to be identified and placed at the top of the 'wish' list. They will obviously require more extensive scrutiny during your product selection.

Functions of a fourth generation language

The capabilitioes of a functionally rich fourth-generation language might include the following: non-procedural language with 'high level' commands; procedural logic; exit capability to existing code; query handling; report generation; internal database management system; relational capability; prototyping facilities; interface to other database management systems; record maintenance; data entry facilities; library maintenance facilities; internal dictionary; interface to other dictionaries; interpretive and compiled language capabilities; financial modelling; graphics; and security, backup and recovery facilities. This is by no means an exhaustive list, but it does give some indication as to what is on offer. It also highlights the importance of understanding what each of these facilities can do for your organisation.

Security and backup are always important

It is often said that fourth-generation languages tend to be weak in the area of security, backup and recovery, so these areas should be closely scrutinised. It is always worth spending some time understanding all the strengths and weaknesses of security, backup and recovery for the 4GL that is on the short list, bearing in mind the importance of these facilities to your organisation or application.

Who will be affected

It is often thought that after determining the objectives and selecting the language which best meets the needs of the organisation the battle is largely won. Yet we have already seen that a project using traditional languages risks failure if it does not adequately address the implementation needs of the application user. The same applies to projects based on fourth-generation languages: if they are not properly implemented they can and do fail. It is therefore useful to examine some of the more important implementation issues which relate to fourth-generation languages. If a fourth-generation language is to be introduced successfully, management guidelines are required. These guidelines must give details of the technical limitations as well as the many beneficial features. These are necessary in order to optimise the design of the system to ensure maximum efficiency.

Dangers of 'de-skilling'

Many fourth-generation languages can be used without employing skilled programmers. However, it is always advisable to ensure that a small number of senior DP staff obtain an understanding of the fourth-generation languages used in order that programs – whether written by users or programming staff – can be critically reviewed to improve their efficiency. This is a service that DP departments should gladly give to the end user.

Documentation is still important

In some installations the documentation never gets done. Often a production line is established for the use of programmers, and jobs for coding are queued until the programmer is free. This maximises the use of the programmer (the scarcest resource) but further adds to the overall time lapse. It does not satisfy the real requirements of the organisation.

In typical, well-controlled installations with a development standard manual, there are about 10 pages of program documentation for every 1000 lines of code.

If a system using 4GLs is going to be used for a considerable length of time and by a number of people it is necessary to ensure that adequate documentation is provided. All small stand-alone fourth-generation language applications demand the same level of specification, documentation and testing as a major 4GL project. It is a necessary discipline and it also provides useful documentation. Although many fourth-generation languages are self-documenting, it is still necessary to ensure that this routine has been carried out. If DP management adequately addresses all of these concerns, then the implementation will usually be successful.

The use of prototyping

In many applications, prototypes should be created quickly in order to find out if the user likes them. The prototyping should be rapidly changeable. It is this facility of fourth-generation languages that is so invaluable. In this environment it is vital that the application creator works hand in hand with the application user. The systems analyst who learns to understand the user's needs should himself create the application and work with the user to adjust it interactively. The other approach is to let the end user do all the work with reference (when necessary) to the DP professionals.

Delays create problems

At the moment the user sees a delay of years before work starts on the applications he needs. The time between specifying requirements and obtaining results can be so long that the requirements have changed in the interim. Many end users are now beginning to understand what computers can do for them. They do not have any formal method of notifying DP departments of any new requirements because they are overloaded. It is as ridiculous as not going to the doctor with an ailment because he has not cured the previous one – in many cases it might not have been identified!

Errors in analysis become less of a problem when analysts can quickly create the application themselves and the users can check the prototype. Fine tuning is something that can be done easily and interactively.

Changing the development life-cycle

The use of fourth-generation languages changes the traditional application development life-cycle. Formal management of system development using fourth-generation languages requires that certain documents be created and reviewed at an early stage. Three phases of the life-cycle are divided into sub-cycles and checklists. These components of cycles are important for guiding development staff and ensuring that nothing important is forgotten. Management standards associated with the traditional life-cycle have acquired the force of law in many organisations. And yet there are obviously problems associated with the traditional life-cycle.

All these tools and techniques have an immediate impact on the effectiveness of computer use. Any one of them would change the historical life-cycle. Each day the life-cycle needs to be re-examined to maximise the degree of automation of system engineering. It is vital to build in data modelling, which is often independent of specific projects; to ensure flexibility so that systems can be easily changed when necessary; and to employ prototyping to ensure that user needs are understood and to provide users with facilities for extracting and manipulating the information needed.

There are several life-cycles that are found in use with fourth-generation languages:

(1)   Ad hoc system
Users or analysts extract or create data, manipulate it, do calculations, build spreadsheets and so on. There is no requirement analysis or written specification. Such systems are maintained by the creator or not at all. There is no formal life-cycle. Much valuable user-driven computing is done this way.

(2)   Prototype cycle
The prototype is built by systems analysts and given to the user. The user reacts to the prototype and calls the systems analyst to modify it. Numerous versions of the prototype may be created until the user is satisfied with it. The prototype then becomes the working system and the analysts may improve its documentation, preferably with on-line help and training aids.

(3)   Prototype 3GL cycle
A prototype is created and redefined as in (2), but is then reprogrammed with a 3GL to achieve greater machine efficiency. The disadvantage of doing this is that the 4GL cannot be used for making quick modifications. We would prefer to have a 4GL with an optimising compiler and a database or a file system designed for machine efficiency.

(4)   Specification on 4GLs cycle
Requirements analysis and specification writing are done as with the traditional development life-cycle and the code is created with the code generator. This pattern is used with complex systems where very careful attention to specification is required (highly integrated manufacturing systems, for example). For machine efficiency the 4GL may be used for only part of the system, or two types of 4GL may be used, one that provides tight

coding and one that provides flexible output.

(5) Specification language cycles

The disadvantage of case (4) is that the manual specification is usually inconsistent, ambiguous, incomplete and prone to misinterpretation. The use of specification languages that develop into specifications is a possibility. However, the specification language should be computable and have a code generator.

To all these patterns of life-cycle we can add one further important consideration – has data modelling been done before the cycle begins? In the fourth-generation environment it is highly advantageous to have thorough data administration. The data administration should maintain the data model as defined by the dictionary and describe the data used in the organisation. Automated tools are used for building the data model. Subsets of data are extracted for individual projects.

At the start of a major project it is desirable to sketch out the life-cycle appropriate to the problem in hand and the tools available.

Information Engineering

The term *information engineering* is used to describe the combination of data modelling and the use of fourth-generation languages to build a computerised system. The building blocks of information engineering are a set of integrated methodologies which need standardised tools and ought to be the formal basis of fourth-generation standards and procedures for DP departments.

When organisations first try out application development using fourth-generation languages, they should be aware of the risks from 'culture shock'. Experienced programmers and analysts find it difficult to unlearn old techniques for the fourth-generation environment, and to overcome this, organisations should select employees who have the ingenuity to adapt to new techniques quickly, and employ graduates from business schools and polytechnics to work with them. The change in DP culture can then be brought about by setting up separate channels for development, employing graduates who are strongly motivated to learn new techniques, and obtaining results with them as quickly as possible.

These new channels should be managed by highly innovative DP professionals who understand the new methods, can make them work and are aware of their limitations. The information centre should be managed by entirely separate channels of DP development.

Chapter Seven
DP Department's Guide to Fourth-Generation Languages under DOS and UNIX

Few DP departments, at first thought, would consider using DOS or UNIX to develop application programs with a 4GL. They would be wrong to dismiss the idea. There are many types of fourth-generation language for the DOS and UNIX environment on the market. But how can they best be used? There is no point in buying a new productivity tool if it is not correctly implemented. So what criteria should the DP professional use when choosing one? The first and most important question to ask is 'What is the application environment?' Different fourth-generation languages are designed for different application environments. A list of some questions (developed from James Martin) that should be asked in connection with a particular application and the associated 4GL are provided below:

- Is it intended for use by the user (possibly in an information centre environment), by the DP professional or by both?
- Is it in an environment with meticulous specification, or one where the tools will be used in an ad hoc, dynamically changeable fashion?
- Is it for batch processing, routine terminal-based computing or exploratory unpredictable computing?
- Is it for commercial data processing or for scientific, engineering, or complex logic computing?
- Will it be used for decision support computing? If so, what categories of decision – simple spreadsheets and graphic operations, or decisions needing sophisticated algorithms?
- Is it needed for heavy duty computing or low transaction volumes?
- Is it intended for a personal computer, a mini-computer, a mainframe environment or a combination of all three?
- What are the data volumes? Are they more than, say, 10 gigabytes, medium-sized or small enough to fit on a PC?

- Will it be used to access existing databases or files? If so, what type? Will it access the existing data on-line or will the data be extracted for its use?
- Will it be used for systems with extremely complex specification, such as large military or aerospace systems?
- Will it be used to build a prototype, the final application, or possibly both?
- Will it be used in conjunction with application packages to increase their flexibility, or to add decision support capability?
- Will it be extended to link up with the functions of the office automation work-station, including text processing, electronic mail, electronic filing, and office management applications?

The answers to these questions will direct the DP department towards the correct 4GL for the particular task. There are a number of other factors that must be taken into consideration. These include the choice of hardware, adherence to new standards, the choice of applications and the management of development staff and users.

4GLs demand extra computing power

The use of fourth-generation languages puts extra demand on computer processing and storage space. There are many reasons for this increase, and if they are understood the possibility of problems occuring will be decreased.

Hardware utilisation
In a 3GL environment the hardware loading is predictable well in advance of the requirement. The need for computer enhancement can be foreseen, since it is related to the advent of a new system. In a 4GL environment the management of computer loading becomes much more critical.

The inefficiency of the 4GL
Most 4GLs, but by no means all, make greater demands on the hardware. This means they often require more power than 3GLs to carry out the same tasks. This has to be taken into consideration, and means that hardware utilisation becomes an important management function.

Fast system development
The use of 4GLs results in the application software being developed much faster than is the case using traditional 3GLs. This improvement in programming productivity means that more systems will be loaded onto the hardware within a given planning period than was previously possible. Many experienced DP professionals have been caught out by this increase.

On-line systems

Since the majority of 4GL development will be used for on-line information retrieval systems, the amount of on-line work will obviously increase. Compared with batch processing this type of system makes much more demand on the computer hardware due to the difficulty of timing the work load. The computer system that is used for an on-line 4GL-developed information system has to be large enough to handle peak loads. It is often difficult to measure the extent of these peak loads accurately but they are invariably larger than planned.

More uncontrolled use

Any on-line application designed for the user will, by its very nature, have more uncontrolled use. This uncontrolled use will create scheduling problems, typically:

- interrogations are made when the user wants them and not when the computer department wants them. This will almost always cause unpredictable peaks.
- users may develop systems without informing the database manager. This could continue, unless controlled, until the computer grinds to a halt.
- user programming may be inefficient, causing, say, the whole database to be searched for simple queries.

Prototyping

Prototyping, the use of incremental development, and all the 'try it and see' methods of feasibility testing and establishing requirements take up considerable additional machine time and storage space. There can be cases when dozens of prototypes for one application may be stored on the computer.

Re-run

The flexibility offered by 4GLs facilitates subsequent changes. There is a tendency for programs to 'go live' faster and with less thorough testing. This tends to increase the number of re-runs (using rapidly corrected versions) due to program failure or failure to get the right information.

All these factors will put more pressure on the computer installation than traditional systems. This has to be taken into account when sizing the system, and when upgrades are planned. The computer system will always have to be much larger when 4GLs are being used. There is always a price to be paid, but since the cost of hardware is decreasing and the number of MIPS one could get in a DOS or UNIX machine per unit cost is higher than in the traditional mainframe environment, the cost should be acceptable.

Standards

It has been suggested that there will be no need for system specifications for the programmers, since there will not *be* any programmers. This is not the case. Salesmen often say there is no need for standards (they are built into the product) or documentation (there is no more maintenance so no one would read it). This is not strictly true either. Developing systems using 4GL have to go through certain stages. If you are building anything, regardless of the tools you use, there has to be *some* kind of plan.

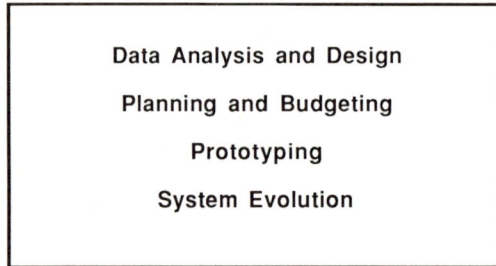

Data Analysis and Design

Planning and Budgeting

Prototyping

System Evolution

Fig. 7.1   Four stages of systems development using 4GLs.

There are four stages in the development of systems using fourth-generation languages

Stage one – data analysis and design
This includes:

- Definition of the application area
- Relationship with corporate objectives
- Data analysis
- Designing the database, access paths and data capture/ data maintenance/ data security strategies. If no database is to be employed this task becomes concerned with main files design.

These are often the major tasks, and a number of methods are used. They usually involve entity analysis and the exploration of one-to-one and one-to-many relationships, with their attributes. Generally speaking *data-driven approaches* (which explore the data implications of the thing being described) appear more suitable for 4GLs using databases, and *goal-driven approaches* (which explore the data implications of achieving the objectives) suit those using separate files.

Stage 2 – Planning and budgeting

- Budget preparation
- Determine development budget period
- Agree system objectives for budget period
- Set out clearly defined user benefits
- Agree systems development and hardware budget

Stage 3 – Prototyping

- Prototype production. Its purpose is to establish the initial systems required and the feasibility of achieving them by trying out ideas using a model. This model is frequently only a simulation of the proposed system and will work only insofar as is necessary to demonstrate outputs and feasibility.

Stage 4 – System evolution

Iterative, bit-at-a-time programming implementation and agreement of new requirements. Standards concerning its use are therefore of great value. In practice standards can cover:

- the purpose
- the type allowed
- the number of iterations allowed.

Documentation standards

Any sensible relaxation of documentation standards is welcome, since (as every DP manager knows) the problem in a 3GL environment is not so much designing good documentation standards as getting them applied. The soundest approach is to question the purpose of documentation; to determine whether each of these purposes is still valid for 4GLs; to define any new purpose relevant to the new techniques; and then to design fresh documentation standards.

Performance standards

This is not an easy task, and will change from one establishment to another, from one application type to another, and from one 4GL to another. It is an area that has to be kept under constant revision. 4GL performance standards are often related to:

- **User satisfaction** (measures of cost versus the achievement of the system and user objectives).
- **Efficiency** (Measure of core occupancy, storage occupancy, CPU time and response times all compared with the budget targets enables the escalation of hardware resources to be effectively controlled).
- **Function points** (measures the functions delivered by the program).

New releases cause problems

The installation of a new 4GL release has to be closely managed. New releases should be tested carefully using an existing program as a 'guinea pig' and adding many of the new features supplied in the release. The situation where satisfactory existing programs suddenly stop or produce incorrect results when new releases are installed is very common.

Choice of application

There are three important areas of concern to management when choosing an application for 4GLs. These are:

- deciding on the suitability of an application for the 4GL
- applications planning and
- reducing the application backlog.

Application types

As a general rule it is important to restrict the use of a 4GL to certain types of application, especially in the first instance. It is advisable to start with the least difficult applications and progress to the more difficult.

A book publisher installed a computer system using a 4GL to achieve rapid systems developments. During the two years they successfully implemented over 50 systems. All their applications made use of 4GL programming techniques. All these systems were small, isolated applications or were constructed as stand-alone systems by extracting ad hoc sub-sets of the database. It proved a successful technique for fast implementation in a new installation – but there may be problems when the company wants to integrate these systems at a later date.

Some general guidelines on applications to avoid

- **Integrated processing**. Stand-alone applications generally fit best with the small systems philosophy of most 4GLs. Intermediate files are often difficult to handle.
- **High transaction volumes**. Inefficiencies in processing speed usually arise when using 4GLs, and can become critical if the application involves high transaction volumes.

One of the main premises when using a fourth-generation language is not dissimilar to the rule for using third-generation languages: 'understand the nature of the application'.

Can 4GLs replace 3GLs completely?

This is a question that all DP managers who are considering 4GLs have to ask. One of the most important considerations when adopting a 4GL is whether you can abandon all future use of a third-generation language such as COBOL or C. In other words, can the 4GL do everything that COBOL can do? There are two aspects to consider. First, does the language have sufficient *functionality* to replace the third-generation language? Second, does the language give *machine performance* good enough to replace a third-generation language? If it does not, is there a cost benefit in providing more machine power?

Number of 'lines of code' is a meaningless measure

The purpose of buying and using a 4GL is to create programs with much less effort than a third-generation language would require. 4GLs vary widely in the degree to which they achieve this objective. A buyer might try to establish a 'COBOL to 4GL ratio' for the number of lines of code produced. Programming needing 1000 lines of COBOL might be written with 50 lines of 4GL. In this case the ratio would be 20. It is nearly impossible to establish a single COBOL to 4GL ratio for most 4GLs. They produce an impressive ratio for certain activities and do much less well with others. The suppliers and sellers tend to select applications that demonstrate the highest COBOL to 4GL ratio. The language might have a high ratio for report generation but a low one for complex logic. An expression based on lines of code is meaningless for many procedural operations, especially those where the user interacts rapidly with the workstation screen. Here the 4GL to COBOL ratio could be more realistically calculated on the relative time taken to create an application. This makes objective measurement still more difficult, because highly trained and skilled 4GL users work much faster than beginners and unskilled users. Hence the industry average for COBOL programmers is about 20 lines of code per day, although many programmers protest that they could code much faster than this.

Chapter Eight
Prototyping – the Key to Success

Fourth-generation languages make it easy to manipulate data and to change the structure of the underlying database. It is this facility that enables prototyping to be used to such good effect. The key to successful implementation of 4GL-based systems is through prototyping. The active participation of the user makes it possible to obtain results without the project being ossified by documentation. Through prototyping, both user and computer specialists can:

- do away with the writing of lengthy and complex system specifications
- improve the product quality
- give (for the first time in this environment) a real-life feedback
- keep the systems dynamic and open to change.

The last point is most important to the numerous systems that are being developed to act as decision support systems. Properly executed, prototyping projects can result in increased efficiency, support short timetables, and assure cost savings and happy users. The classical systems analyst nearly disappears with prototyping because many systems descriptions tasks are performed automatically by the 4GL. An ideal prototyping environment has three components,

(1) the 4GL, to allow quick prototype development
(2) properly managed data resources, from the database to data communication
(3) users and computer professionals knowledgeable in employing the 4GL and structuring the data.

The computer professional is often needed as a prototype builder, although this is not always the case since users can employ these tools to create the prototype themselves. However, the best team to start with will include one user and one business or systems analyst. The user is the person who needs the work done: the computer professional knows the tricks of the trade.

Types of Prototypes   Prototyping Stages

| Throw-it-away Prototyping |
| Evolutionary Prototyping |

| Prototype Objectives |
| Function Selection |
| Prototype Construction |
| Evaluation |

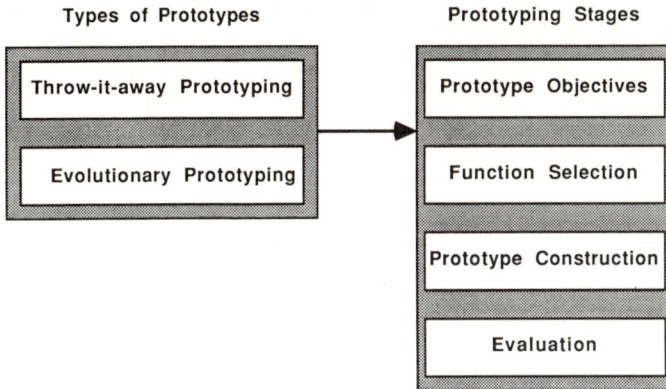

Fig. 8.1   Prototyping.

Three unpleasant facts about the classical development life-cycle

First, the earlier an activity occurs in the development cycle the poorer are the notations used for that activity. Secondly, the earlier an activity occurs in the development cycle the less is understood about the nature of the activity. Finally, the earlier an error is made in the development cycle the more catastrophic the effects of that error.

Unfortunately when a software developer uses modern notations and techniques, success is only likely when the application is both well understood and supported by previous experience. The current rate of growth in hardware acquisition means larger numbers of end users are demanding more new applications each year. In order to develop these systems the old knowledge is inadequate.

Prototyping can tackle some of these problems because of the speed with which a system can be specified and demonstrated. It develops into a means of communication between the DP developer and the user, and enables the user to develop the type of system he requires.

Productivity can come through developing prototypes and not specifications

Let us examine the notions advanced so far. 4GLs offer a chance to break free from the rigidity of traditional approaches: they offer not only faster development but also the opportunity to provide working systems for the user. The key is the ability to adopt an experimental approach to development.

By developing prototype functions instead of specifications, the user is, for the first time, given real-life feedback on what the end results will look like. He can then look at them, control them, alter them and update them without throwing the project six months behind schedule, as happens in the classical development cycle. This highlights some unpleasant facts that face traditional DP staff.

A cultural gap

There is usually a significant cultural gap between the user and the software developer, and it appears in the way they communicate. A user often finds it extremely hard to visualise a system simply by reading a technical systems specification. DP staff, on the other hand, have great difficulty in writing these documents. If the customer is unable to visualise a system then validation during the early part of the software project becomes a very error-prone process. This cultural gap also means that the user unfamiliar with information technology may have produced very vague requirements which could be interpreted arbitrarily by the developer.

Evidence suggests that once a user starts employing a computer system, changes occur in his ideas about what the system should do; this invalidates the original requirements. As a result, user requirements are often a moving target, and producing a system that meets them is a risky and error-prone activity. A further complication is that a software project of considerable size may take many years to complete. During this time the user requirements, as well as the user's environment, may have changed considerably, making a complete system even more obsolete.

Prototype development

It is not always clear exactly what is meant by prototyping in the context of software engineering. Some insist that the term should refer to a 'mock' version, a system which can be thrown away after use. Others suggest that a prototype may become the final system by a process of continual improvement, matching the system to the user's needs. To avoid confusion these are identified as two separate approaches, the 'throw-it-away' approach and 'evolutionary development'.

Throw-it-away prototyping

The need for rapid development is greatest in throw-it-away prototyping.

Since the prototype is to be used for a limited period, quality factors of the product (e.g. efficiency, structure, maintainability, full error handling and documentation) are of little relevance. The prototype may be implemented on target hardware or, more likely, on an environment other than that required for the target system, such as a personal computer. However, what is important is that the prototype should be constructed with evaluation in mind. It should therefore address only those aspects required in any objective evaluation.

Evolutionary prototyping

Evolutionary prototyping, on the other hand, is in complete contrast to the throw-it-away approach and in complete antithesis to traditional software development methods. Proponents of this strategy argue that information systems have to evolve steadily by their very nature, thereby invalidating the original requirements. The purpose of the evolutionary approach is to introduce the system into the organisation, allowing it to adapt to inevitable change.

Evolutionary prototyping is by far the most powerful way of coping with the changes that occur in any dynamically oriented business environment. This approach requires the system to be designed in such a way that it can cope with change during – and, more importantly, *after* – development. A design practice that does not take the possibility of change into account can and does lead to severe problems.

Main difference between this and the traditional approach

The main difference between this approach and conventional software development is that it is highly iterative and dynamic. During each iteration respecification, redesign, re-implementation and re-evaluation take place. As a result, the impact of early errors is much less serious. Furthermore, the initial version of the system is delivered very early during the software project.

The dynamic nature of this approach is a major challenge both to the developer and the user. Success often depends not only on an effective means of designing an adaptable system but also on the willingness of both sides to open themselves up to communication and change for a significant period.

Prototyping consists of four stages:

(1) The establishment of prototyping objectives
It is essential to establish what a prototype is supposed to be used for and what

aspects of a proposed system it should reflect. A clear statement of the lessons that are expected to be learnt from the prototype is also required.

(2)   Function selection
A prototype usually covers only those aspects of the system from which the required information may be obtained. The selection of the functions to be included in the prototype should be directly influenced by the prototype objectives. Depending on these objectives, prototyping may be carried out horizontally, vertically or diagonally.

(3)   Prototype construction
Of great importance is the speed and cost of prototype construction. Fast, low-cost construction is normally achieved by ignoring the normal quality requirements for the final product unless, of course, they are in conflict with the objectives.

(4)   Evaluation
This is the most important step in the prototyping process and must be carefully planned. The users of the system must have been given proper training, and resources should be made available for evaluation sessions. The evaluation process should be controlled through the use of meaningful measures. During evaluation, inconsistencies and shortcomings in the developer's perception of customer requirements are uncovered. Many features of the system may prove unexpected or inadequate to the user.

During the evaluation of a prototype the customer effectively learns about a proposed system and his own needs. At the same time the developer learns about the way the customer conceives a problem. The prototype becomes an effective communication medium which enables the two parties to learn about each other without requiring them to have an in-depth knowledge of each other's fields. The feedback obtained from the evaluation phase must be studied, recorded and used effectively to improve the prototype.

Some problems always remain

During the prototype process the user is unlikely to identify all the remaining problems in the system through a single evaluation phase. The prototype usually needs to be modified and subjected to further evaluation. The process is carried out iteratively until the prototype is commensurate with a reasonably stable set of requirements. The time between iterations is extremely important. Good, timely feedback is essential for productive learning.

Management issues

The role of management in a software project of any size is crucial. A software project that employs prototyping is not an exception. Unfortunately, current literature on the subject often ignores managerial issues. Two problems arise, both of which are purely educational. First, a development strategy based on prototyping challenges the management tradition of an organisation, and effectively requires different methods of management. To overcome this, training has to be given and management has to have an understanding of the power and purpose of fourth-generation languages and the importance of prototyping.

Secondly, it may also prove a challenge to the development team. Many new skills have to be learnt and, more importantly, a totally new way of providing solutions has to be developed.

The changes required to current software project management practice in order to incorporate either the throw-away or the evolutionary approach should not be too difficult to make, provided there is willingness on all sides. This is because both approaches are compatible with the current phase-oriented approach to software development. However, the impact of the evolutionary approach on current project management practice is far greater. In most organisations very few real-life projects have been based on this approach, and there is often a reluctance to start something new. However, this is a problem that has to be tackled by all managers, DP and user. By taking this approach a number of managerial issues will be uncovered. This is in direct contrast with, say, the throw-away approach where (for example) it is now acknowledged that 10% to 20% of the total budget should be allocated to this phase.

A sensible solution to managing an evolutionary approach

Probably the most sensible solution to managing evolutionary prototyping projects is to make the management as dynamic as the development process itself. One promising suggestion is to adopt a dynamic contract strategy: contracts are formalised but regularly negotiated during the development process.

However, no strict rules should be laid down for the way in which the prototype is built. This is often best left to the temperament of the analyst/ programmer. Past experience makes it apparent that even when code from different programmers implements the same function, there is hardly a line in common between the two versions. There is little chance of using one source level definition of the abstract algorithm to generate another. This example not only illustrates a loss of portability due to the programmer's temperament but also points to a situation where 4GLs and prototyping can be of help.

To achieve this, the properties of the information object are defined by relying on a sample representation of it, and also by linking this very process to the computer and the compiler. Several 4GLs work through metaphors, i.e. ways of describing what the computer is doing as contrasted to what people do. A metaphor helps in alluding to actions such as sending a message or providing an interface with common technology.

Prototyping to follow the data structure approach

Prototyping can follow either *functional decomposition* or, preferably, *data structure* approach. These are the two schools of thought developed since the mid 1970s for structured systems design and analysis. The latter is more recent, and helps solve some tough problems. First, it is difficult to find the best way to implement a decomposing function. It is even more difficult to reconcile the function structure with the data structure. Although the automation of functional decomposition has resulted in many new tools, including application generators and definition languages, the success of those tools pales when compared with the results that can be obtained with a 4GL along data structure lines. In the mid 1970s, tools started becoming available that increased the systems analyst's productivity through structured approaches. The focus on increasing the vigour of functional decomposition, however, led to much bureaucracy in system design, and that, in turn, increased project costs and lead time. The evidence can be seen by observing the massive tomes needed to provide guidance methodologies.

Decomposition strategies seemed especially weak in the face of the changes occurring in the whole concept of information management.

These changes are evidenced by the wide acceptance of database management systems and end-user computing. At the same time, facilities supported through 4GLs have been instrumental in increasing software quality. This is particularly valuable to professionals because computer programs are governed by Murphy's Law – any system eventually comes down.

To summarise, prototyping can be of great value in two specific cases:

(1) When the user is not sure of his or her needs. A visual programming approach helps clarify those needs by providing a test bed for the description of the system. The prototype acts as the breadboard model of the application.
(2) When the computer professional wants to experiment in order to optimise the design, file, and code structure. Optimisation can only be done by specialists who are well versed in the use of development tools,

concerned about the use of resources, aware of short response time needs, and able to understand the organisation's information requirements.

Prototyping and software quality

The object of a prototype is to help put in concrete form the structure and design functionality of a system, while leaving the issue of optimisation open. For this reason prototyping tools may take specifications at some level of abstraction (such as 'definition of requirements') and transform them into operational views. This approach enables users to examine the implications of specifications in the real world. Here they can interact with the system they have specified in their requirements.

Properties of the initial prototype

An initial early prototype must be produced quickly and cheaply, present an accurate reflection of the specification, ensure a faithful representation of the system and maintain consistency between prototype and evolving specifications. This is what a fourth-generation language can help to accomplish. Once the prototype has shown its feasibility, optimisation can be attacked.

In other words, programming work should be done through an executable requirement language, and this language should be formalised for functional modelling. The 4GL chosen should be one that can implement the specification efficiently and quickly. The use of standard re-usable components should provide an approximation of the desired system. At the current state of the art we look for a solution through the synthesis of different programming tools. We know that it is difficult because of the different philosophies, assumptions, levels, notations and so on that different programming tools employ. We also appreciate the need to define a conceptual as well as a notional base for such an aggregate of tools.

5GLs – the next set of productivity tools

By the end of the decade we can expect fifth-generation languages (5GLs) based on artificial intelligence. Artificial intelligence is concerned with knowledge organisation and structuring. The experience and feedback of using 4GLs, coupled with the massive R&D effort in artificial intelligence, will ensure a progressive move towards 5GLs. Currently, third-generation languages are applied to static systems; the next step is to extend software tools to include the solution of the far wider area of dynamic systems.

Dynamic systems will necessitate the technology of fifth-generation computing.

We are not yet at that point. Today, we have a methodology, and tools for analysis and specification – that is an improvement on the tools of yesterday. Let us forget that requirement deficiencies are largely responsible for cost overruns and quality problems. In practice, requirement specification errors are normally not detected until integrated spot tests are carried out, or the operational phase of the software life-cyle is reached. At that point they are expensive to correct. 4GLs can be used as a prototyping tool to help the analyst design a system, and can also be used to provide alternative views of system requirements.

Computer used as an analysis tool

With 4GLs the computer is used as an analysis tool in specifying requirements. Fourth-generation languages are interactive: they provide for easy and rapid access to requirement information in a variety of forms. They also have an underlying formal model basis for communicating with user and designer.

By supporting prototyping, 4GLs make it possible to reduce the impact of specification changes. They allow documentation to be automatically modified, and provide a computer-supported testbed. With manual approaches, the programs rely on intimate knowledge of the program and its strengths and weaknesses. Device tests are used to attack the weak points. This task is difficult, and the programmer is often reluctant to attack his own code and try to make it fail. Many programmers deliberately avoid testing areas they know to be weak. One of the great advantages of program generators is that they make it possible to design program testing that takes advantage of the program's generated structure, test boundaries, and other conditions.

The current situation can be improved

To improve the current situation, a production process must be improved in a way that allows little or no chance for analysts and programmers to make mistakes. Part of the solution is to ensure that any feedback is able to adjust itself. The proper, computer-based implementation of feedback can see to it that programming products are not only free from faults, but also satisfy other criteria of software quality. Quite evidently structured approaches and feedbacks are tantamount to introducing a new methodology and tools and rearranging the process accordingly. It is equally vital for the software producer to digest such improvements. Because they are computer-based and permit a steady feedback, 4GLs offer great improvements over existing systems. The latter are frequently inadequate to allow sufficient modification and upgrading of software in the field.

Software maintenance has classically been flawed by poor design practices, non-existent or outdated documentation, lack of requirement or design data, and inadequate test data. Deficiencies in the design process generally result in a long list of user complaints ranging from the need for redesign and reprogramming to two-level bug correction. Prototyping helps correct this situation by presenting the user with a version of information handling as it would be in the real world. The subsequent modifications may be vast, but can be accomplished quite easily using a 4GL.

Through prototyping we can develop tools that are designed to transfer into the maintenance phase. We can also obtain the necessary database or design information, configuration management, and test results. Since this information is already available, there is an orderly transition into the maintenance phase of the development process. The common result of these benefits is software quality. To appreciate that, we must speak of the basic criteria needed to evaluate the quality of the programming products: reliability, operability, efficiency and maintainability.

A valid comparison is with the way the Japanese software developers approach the issue. Prototyping creates a different cycle of DP development from the traditional one. The first step is the broad determination of what the user needs. Often the user makes a request, an analyst studies it, determines what data is required, and then determines how it might be prototyped. For a small system this can be informal (without any written specification). For a larger system it might involve a detailed written description of what data is needed, and data flow diagrams or action diagrams showing how the database will be used.

In the second step a working prototype is created. It is important that this is done quickly. The prototype may use the standard default option or a non-procedural facility or data management system in order to demonstrate something to the user quickly. Initially it may demonstrate only the major functions; it will not yet include peripheral details, auditors' requirements and so on.

Prototyping seems so vital to the development process and has saved so much money in maintenance that it is amazing so many systems are still developed without prototypes. DP managers seem reluctant to change their methods and lack education about the tools now available. In our view there is no data processing system that should not be prototyped or built with a 4GL, either partially or completely. There have been too many catastrophes, too many unhappy users, and too much maintenance expense for anyone to assume it is safe to go into a lengthy and expensive third-generation development without the up front reality testing that prototypes provide. When the user works with prototypes for a few weeks, he almost always improves the resulting system.

A major criticism of prototyping is that it is in antithesis to the need for discipline on the software project. This may well be a myth. A number of authors have stressed that the need for discipline on a prototpying project is as high as on any other project, and its enforcement is the responsibility of management.

Another important issue concerns the way the development team for prototyping is organised and operated. Suggestions include:

- Keeping the prototyping team as small as possible. This facilitates better communication, cuts down the documentation effort, and enables faster iterations between each prototype.
- In choosing team members for a prototyping project give preference to those who have had previous experience with the prototyping approach.
- Making sure that the team members are willing to cooperate with users as well as each other. The reward system adopted for the project should take this into account and encourage cooperation.

Management should also ensure that the following points are taken into account

- The provision of sufficiently powerful tools to aid prototyping strategy
- Commitment to user training courses to introduce users to the prototype system.

Chapter Nine
Training for 4GLs

Technology and human skills

In order to gain the maximum benefit from fourth-generation languages, there is an overwelming need to develop and increase the skills base available within the organisation. An improved skills base has to be provided both for the DP staff (who are going to be involved with these new productivity tools) and for the users. This is proving to be a difficult task, for a number of reasons. The biggest stumbling block is that there is no base worth talking about on which to build the new skills. For the user, the office-based knowledge worker has been the most under-trained sector of the workforce. Compared with the training given to skilled and semi-skilled blue-collar workers, or lavished on members of the armed forces, the amount available to the office worker is meagre in the extreme. This is one reason why the productivity of the office worker has been so small. Although the new breed of fourth-generation languages are very easy to use, training must be given in order to obtain the maximum benefit and obtain the highest level of productivity possible.

DP staff are not much better

As with many office workers, most DP staff just do not have the training for the jobs they are expected to do. This is a bleak judgement of many specialists in system development and methodology. How the powers that be can expect their organisations to exploit the new and exciting computer-related developments is a mystery. Both DP staff and users require training.

DP staff must become business-oriented

The training currently available to DP staff has not taken account of the changed roles needed within the organisation. DP departments still train their staff in what is termed the 'bottom up' method. A programmer's training, for example, will typically encompass only the minutiae of programming syntax: good programmers are then trained in the slightly wider field of systems design: and with luck they are then trained to become systems analysts. On each rung of the ladder, DP staff are trained to take a relatively narrow view of the task they are asked to do. Few programmers have any understanding of the business area which is the focus of the project they are working on. How, then can they develop the necessary rapport with the user? The same is true of many analysts working on a project. Their understanding of the role and significance of the business area within the company they are working for is often abysmal.

Even at the higher level, how many head DP managers are as well-versed in the culture or overall objectives of the company as their business peers in other departments? The DP staff are a service function for the whole organisation, and as such they should have an understanding of what the company does, how their skills fit into the overall pattern, and what additional skills they require in order to improve their service to the organisation.

The major problems facing many DP departments today do not only relate to failures in programming and design techniques. They also relate to their failure to understand the fundamental nature of business. If they really understood the requirements of the business, they would surely realise the necessity to change their working methods to meet those requirements.

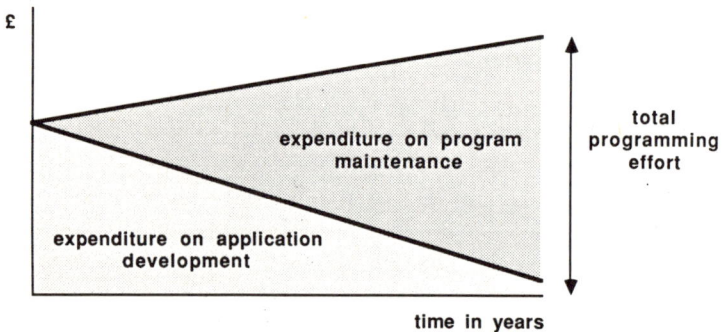

Note: some corporations spend 80% of their programming budget on maintenance and only 20% on new projects.

Fig. 9.1 Cost escalation of system development using third generation languages.

Current DP training does nothing to equip DP staff to perform successful business analysis or to provide a department with strategy optimisation to benefit their business to the utmost. Much of a DP personnel's time (and some estimates have put it at upwards of 80%), is spent correcting existing systems. This will hardly produce the excitement and understanding needed to develop new solutions for companies striving to project their products and services in a competitive environment. DP staff must be trained to meet the business challenges of today, not to be 'medics' armed only with sticking plaster.

Maintenance men rarely develop into innovative designers

A profession, let alone a department, that spends the majority of its time maintaining existing systems is not ideally placed to help an organisation to use computers and software in an effective and innovative manner. When they are not correcting programming errors, they are trying to rectify systems that have been analysed and designed incorrectly. Analysts frequently fail to understand the nature of the business their systems are supposed to support. There have been attempts to remedy the situation, but still the majority of personnel in the DP department have to spend their time tearing the guts out of these systems and putting them back together again. The situation is clear. If DP staff don't understand business, then the chances are that they will get most of their systems wrong – in some cases horrendously and expensively wrong.

£100 at Analysis Stage   £10,000 at Implementation Stage

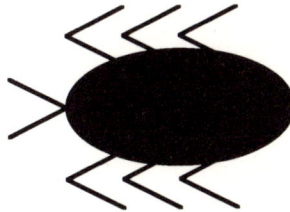

Fig. 9.2   Cost of bug fixing.

Figures from IBM indicate that a problem costing £100 to fix during analysis costs £10,000 to fix after implementation. Other sources indicate that 70% of the cost of an application during its life is spent on maintenance. In other words, if it costs £30,000 to develop a system, it will cost £70,000 to maintain it. This, of course, is using 3GLs, with all their inflexibilities and built-in problems. Demand for more formal methods of developing computer systems is being fuelled by such statistics, since this is the 'logical' route for those trapped in the thought process associated with 3GLs and traditional computing.

Training is the key

All this ties back to the overall point about training. A large proportion of the problems faced by DP staff can be laid squarely at the door of training, or rather lack of training. In the same way, many of the methods DP staff use were developed from the bottom up. Structured programming methods such as the Jackson method were initiated first. These were followed by structured design methods. Finally analysis methods such as 'data flow' were developed. This only goes to confirm that DP staff have been trained from the bottom up. Programmers are turned into designers, who then become analysts, who then try to become business analysts – and so on. All the time, DP staff are trained to think in an exquisitely sequential manner. First do this, then do that. They don't stop to think of the wider implications of what they are doing.

In the context of new methodologies oriented towards information engineering, that approach to training simply isn't good enough. It must be hammered home again and again that the problem of DP arises not only from a failure to cope with technical matters, but also directly from the failure to understand the wider implications of business. In reality it doesn't matter if the programs you write represent the pinnacle of the software engineer's art. If the analyst specifying the program doesn't understand the business area the program is intended to support, that program will be of little real use to the business. We need to completely alter the training perspective of DP staff to take methodologies oriented towards information engineering into account.

DP staff must be trained from the *top down*, and begin by learning the nature of business itself. There is a need to immerse DP staff in the business culture of the specific company for which they are working. They should know how the company makes its money, who its competitors are, what determines its success, how the company is structured, why the structure has been developed in this manner, where it is going and how it is going to get there.

This does not just mean the usual two-day trainee induction course; it is much more fundamental than that. Understanding the overall nature of the business in general and of the company in particular is as important to an analyst as learning how to draw data-flow diagrams. In the future, as more and more of the development processes become automated via the use of work benches, it will become infinitely more important. It has to be remembered that most computer systems effectively alter the culture of the business area they are automating. The larger the system, the larger the cultural change. How can an analyst hope to understand the degree of change effectively unless he or she is deeply immersed in the business culture in the first place? This is basically a plea for lateral thinking in the DP department, and undoubtedly these changes will come sooner rather than later. It may not, however, come as a result of changed attitudes among the DP staff. It may be that the development of easy-to-use productivity tools such as 4GLs will result in the demise of the DP department and the growth of business staff who can program computers.

Already a number of organisations are reporting that it is easier to teach non-technical staff the techniques of business methodology than to convert DP staff from 'bottom up' to 'top down' thinking. One PC software house which specialises in fourth-generation techniques has already ceased recruiting new staff from DP backgrounds, preferring instead to take on solid outsiders. That is a trend that ought to worry most DP staff and the people who train them. This change will not come about without well-planned training, both for the user and DP staff.

The need to train human resources

The tools are there, but are we ready to use them? Can users and computer professionals absorb all the new developments and breakthroughs? While some corporations and organisations make efforts to keep their information systems as advanced as possible, others deliberately hang back. They are overwhelmed by the massive need to retrain and update their human resources.

Training in the new technologies is an overwhelming task. Yet there is plenty of evidence that without massive training and subsequent hands-on implementation the gains from 4GLs will be limited. It is no use just thinking about the tremendous productivity gains that *can* be obtained, there must be a positive and active effort to train and upgrade the skills of all staff.

It is because technology moves so fast and market orientation changes that an organisation must always be on the alert. If an organisation has a good system that is not updated to reflect market changes, it will become inefficient surprisingly fast. This leads to labour-intensive tasks. The same thing is true of personnel. In short, we must organise for knowledge management. In businesses that deal with information and knowhow, management has to cope with a new phenomenon: a rapidly developing divergence between

- power based on position and
- power based on knowledge.

This divergence occurs because the base of knowledge that constitutes the foundation of any business changes every day. An extreme example is in the

City (money and stock markets). It is not surprising that this sector of the market has invested heavily in computerisation and that City firms are avid users of all productivity tools. If the organisation sticks to old-fashioned methods of making decisions, decisions will be made by people unfamiliar with the technology of the day. This is likely to result in poor and possibly costly decisions being made. In general, the faster the change in the knowhow on which the business depends, the greater the divergence between knowledge and power. This highlights the need to train the user to use the computer power available and anticipate ways that computer power can be used to enhance future business situations.

Training will vary depending on the type of 4GL used

The training required will vary with the type of 4GL used. A highly specialised 4GL, spreadsheet analysis for example, can be learnt from a manual, whereas a general-purpose procedural language for DP professionals needs to be taught on a course – and then refined in its use by on-the-job training. The training facilities required should first be identified. These requirements can then be used as a yardstick to evaluate the training facilities provided when choosing a product. There are seven main methods of training:

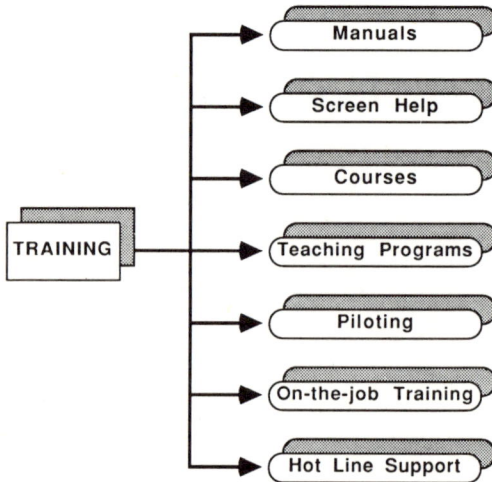

Fig. 9.3 Training methods.

(1) **Manuals.** A manual describing how to get started and the use of all the features available should always be provided.

(2) **Screen help.** A help facility is often provided in the 4GL itself. This gives information about the facilities and how to use them in a more readily available form than a manual.

(3) **Courses.** Training courses are sometimes provided by the supplier. Charges for training vary, and are often negotiable at the time of purchase. The length of these training courses can vary from one day to two weeks or more. It is important to examine the course objectives; some are introductory, some attempt to cover all facilities, and some are 'cut-down' courses for users. The level of skill and experience required of participants should also be investigated.

(4) **Teaching programs.** Self-teach facilities may be provided in the form of teaching programs. These run on the hardware to be used by the 4GL and take the intended user through a planned training course. Usually they include progress checks on comprehension. The advantage of these methods is that in addition to providing flexibility in scheduling training they are frequently built round the 4GL itself, and thus offer 'hands-on' experience under controlled conditions throughout the course.

(5) **Piloting.** The possibility of carrying out trials of the product before purchase can be very useful. A pilot exercise may also be run after the product is chosen, specifically for the purpose of training. In either case, the provision of special training courses and the secondment of an experienced advisor to the 'pilot' team should be investigated with the prospective suppliers.

(6) **On-the-job training.** Every product, no matter how simple, will require some on-the-job training. It may be possible to treat this informally, with users having access to a manual or an experienced in-house person when they get stuck or need a short exercise to improve their skills. When using the more powerful 4GLs, however, continued access to the supplier must be assured.

(7) **Hot line support.** A hot line support facility, either provided by the supplier or developed in-house, is a useful training facility.

Find out what the supplier can provide

The importance of training and the support available from the supplier cannot be emphasised too much. An example of the need to check the experience of the supplier is shown by a printing and publishing company who had no experience of computer-based stock control. They wished to set up a simple system to track stocks of books and periodicals. After investigating the possibility of using a 4GL to develop the application they selected a product that was backed by a large company. The product had been developed in the US, where the great majority of its users were located. Unfortunately the supplier did not have experience in the UK and could only give general advice. The training was based on a description of the 'language' and not on how to use it. The UK supplier was unable to answer simple questions, and in the end the publishing company was teaching the UK supplier about the product and how to use it. Fortunately the 4GL in question was very robust, and the developers at the publishing house very determined, which resulted in a useful system being developed. However, it would have been a lot easier with proper training and support.

Different people need different types of training

There are not only different training methods but also different *types* of training. Two distinct types of training are usually required for technicians and end-users.

Technicians

If the product is intended for use by programmers, training must be pitched at the appropriate level for people with experience or programming aptitude. If the product is intended for users, then special training in its use (providing insights into how it works) should be given to the technicians who are to support the users.

End-users

If the product is intended for users, training should assume no computer knowledge and be designed to take the mystique out of the subject. It is of particular importance to distinguish these two types of training when 'two-tier' 4GLs are being used – these are designed for use both by professionals and by users.

An example of the difference between the two types of training can be shown by the experience of a shoe and leather goods manufacturer. They reported a success with the use of a 4GL by their systems development staff, but an initial failure when they tried to introduce the product to the users. Although the product offered special, easy-to-use features, there was no 'user-tailored' training course provided by the suppliers. The users were sent on the programmers' course. As a consequence they believed that they could not use the product because it was too difficult. However, once the company devised its own user course, which took the user through each subject individually, the users gained confidence and are now enthusiastic about the language.

Training costs money, but it is not as expensive as failure to train. In the future a lot more training will have to take place to help users utilise fourth-generation languages and productivity tools profitably. If they don't, organisations will have only themselves to blame for the results.

Chapter Ten
Computer Languages and Future Developments

There has been and will continue to be a tremendous amount of interest in the developments associated with expert systems and the fifth generation of computer languages. This is very understandable, since they are expected to open up exciting opportunities in all areas of computing. However, before everyone gets carried away with the possibilities, it is important to realise that today's computer-based systems can only be created using the tools that are available at present. Moreover, even if the fifth-generation languages were available there would be very sound reasons for caution.

Understanding the pattern of technological development

The process of developing computer systems involves the use of technology, so an understanding of technology is required. This is far more complex than one might first imagine. Even industries and workplaces where technology has been a common feature over the years, such as the manufacturing industries, find it difficult to come to terms with new computerised technology. Motor manufacturers, steel mills, and most strikingly the print workshops of Fleet Street have all had difficulties developing their industries using computerised technology. Since many of the new computer languages, whether fourth or fifth generation, will be used in the office by non-computer personnel, it is important to understand the technical level that has been reached in the office. Before the introduction of the personal computer the office had seen few developments in technology. The most noticeable were the introduction of the ballpoint pen and the photocopier. It is therefore unlikely that office workers will assimilate new technologies and working practices easily.

The introduction of new computer techniques, therefore, is not only a management activity; it also involves technology. Technology has its own life-cycles, patterns and laws. These have to be understood in order to ensure that the correct decisions are made.

Artificial organs – extensions of our natural ones

Technology, as Freud drolly observed, is really a set of artificial organs, extensions of our natural ones. He understood, as many still do not, that the relationship between ourselves and our tools is too often blurred, though it is very intimate. It is a love-hate relationship. Observe how people treat their cars. They will lavish hours of care and attention on the machine, and then be tempted to kick the living daylights out of it when it grinds to a halt on a motorway miles from nowhere. This seems strange: the development of all technologies has been very natural and always totally controlled by man; not by the stars, or the weather, or God, but by man himself.

Do you trust technology?

Although the development of technology is a constant thread in human history, there is a distrust of technology. The question is, why? Is it because we feel that technological development will become ungovernable and ultimately beyond human control? That is certainly the case as far as computers are concerned.

If the control of fire represents one of the first instances of man's mastery of natural forces, then the man who caused the first 'accidental' forest fire must surely be one of the earliest examples of technology out of control. One can imagine that even then, in the prehistoric forests, our ancestors must have had a lively discussion about the continued use of this new discovery, so wonderful, yet so awesome. The optimists must have won out, as optimists usually do. To implement computer systems one must be an optimist.

The modern domestic environment – a monument to technology

Before we examine the effect of new developments in computer languages, let us consider the domestic environment. The main difference between the house of a hundred years ago and that of today is that the modern house contains a great deal of machinery. For a long time the only 'machine' in a British home was a stove. Most of the other kitchen implements were hand tools. The contemporary house, as the architect Le Corbusier remarked, has become 'a machine for living': an environment conditioned primarily by technology in the form of electrical pumps, motors, furnaces, air conditioners, toasters and hairdryers. There are technologies for providing hot and cold water, and for getting rid of it. There are telephone systems and cable television systems: unseen airwaves carry radio and television signals. The house is also full of automated devices – relays and thermostats – which turn these machines on and off, regulate heat and cold, or simply open the garage door. Remove technology from the modern house, and it would be almost uninhabitable. Cut off the power which fuels the machines for long enough and the dwelling has to be evacuated.

Is the office ready for a technological revolution?

Can our offices become like our houses? A household of fifty years ago had servants using basic technology to cook, wash and maintain a house. Now we do without servants by using the latest developments in technology, such as freezers, microwave ovens, automatic central heating, providing a higher standard of service with fewer people. The same will be the case in the office. It should be remembered that the standard of comfort, cleanliness and cuisine is potentially much higher now that servants have been replaced with technology. There is no reason to suppose that when staff are replaced with the latest technology, the standard of service in the office will increase, but first one has to understand how technological development takes place.

The stages of technological development

There are basically three stages of technological development. The first is the *tool stage* – human energy guided by human intellect. The second is the machine stage – human energy replaced by some outside, non-human source, which continues to be guided by human intellect. Finally comes the third stage – the automated machine which guides itself. It is this third stage that the fifth generation of languages are addressing. However, it is important to understand that all technologies follow this example to a greater or lesser extent, be they computer languages or methods of transport. For example, the problem of carrying people was resolved, amongst other things, by the sedan chair (as it came to be called) – human energy and human control. The sedan was then replaced with a horse and cart, and later by a motor vehicle – non-human energy (horse power of one sort or another) and human control. The third stage of automation would be self-guided vehicles or fully automated underground systems – non-human energy and no direct human control.

All developments aim for total automation

The evolution of technology towards automation can be seen everywhere: in the domestic water-heater, the motor car choke, the solar water heater, the self-winding watch or the traffic light. It is curious that automation has been

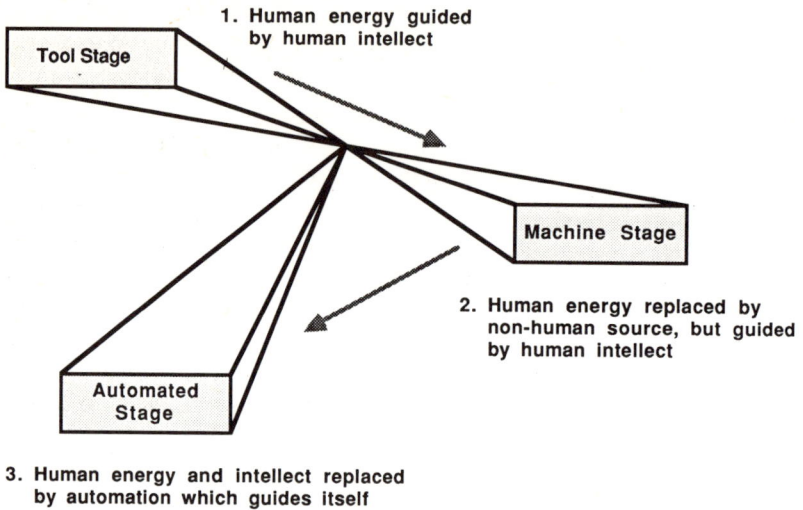

1. Human energy guided by human intellect

Tool Stage

Machine Stage

2. Human energy replaced by non-human source, but guided by human intellect

Automated Stage

3. Human energy and intellect replaced by automation which guides itself

Fig. 10.1 The three stages of technological development.

portrayed as a frightening and unnatural invention: until recently the robot in science-fiction literature has been an ominous, not a chummy character. It is curious because automation is seen in nature. Most of our body is automated, and the desire for automation and the predictability it brings with it is simply the human desire for technology to be as stable as the human heart or as predictable as a sunrise.

One of the main benefits of computerisation will be order and predictability, a feature that is sadly missing from all but the most exceptional traditional commercial environments.

Computer experts, whether they are computer manufacturers, software developers or seasoned practitioners, have a number of characteristics in common. One is the systems approach to problems, and the other is their love of crystal-ball gazing. Being crystal-ball gazers they often fail to take the inherent nature of technological development into account. In their desire to forecast the future they fail to understand that all technological developments since the beginning of time have progressed through clearly defined phases.

Their inability to 'get it right' can be demonstrated by examining the way in which their forecasts for office automation have gone awry. This is an important example. The office is one of the main areas where fourth- and fifth-generation languages will be used, and the technological developments associated with office automation are no different from any other.

In the office the first stage was a quill pen

In the office the first stage in this development pattern was the office worker using a pen or typewriter to put thoughts onto paper. This stage has existed since modern offices were first developed during the 18th century. In the Middle Ages few people outside the Church could write. The amount of business carried out by any one person was limited to the amount he could remember. The most successful people had very good memories! The only type of office work which would be recognised as such today was done by the Church. This mainly consisted of recording deaths and births and registering land transfers.

Since those early times the office has developed in size but not in the technology used. The introduction of the ballpoint pen was the first major development that affected everyone in the office. It was so revolutionary that it was the subject of countless articles, radio programmes and presentations, yet it was still very much part of the first stage of technological development.

The third stage will be a totally automated and paperless system. It is this third stage that most industry watchers have written about and the majority of computer manufacturers have tried to design. It is also the stage at which most of the Department of Trade and Industry office automation pilot studies have been aimed.

In the UK the Department of Trade and Industry funded 21 two-year pilot projects between 1982 and 1985, and the total number of terminals associated with these pilot projects was in the order of 200–300. When these terminals are compared with the 500,000 personal computers installed in the UK in the same period, one has to wonder. Never mind the numbers; just examine the acceptance of these systems compared with that of the personal computer. Few of the DoTI systems have gained any acceptance in the marketplace, yet the majority of these personal computers are used in the office to improve productivity or as office automation machines. The pilot schemes used some of the biggest computer manufacturers in office automation, and yet none of them experienced anything resembling the personal computer's level of acceptance. Why? Did the Department of Trade and Industry back 21 wrong horses? Or did they fail to understand the nature of technological development?

Miss the second stage at your peril

Unfortunately they all missed out the second stage – the machine phase – when they developed their concept of the third stage in office automation. But as technologists they surely should have realised that it is impossible to design the third stage from the first without having the input that the second gives.

They gave themselves an impossible task, and that is why they failed. The technologists who designed and used the sedan chair as a means of transport could not be expected to design a totally automated transport system. If they had tried the results would have been very odd indeed! Some of the attempts to produce an automated office have also been odd! The failures might have been a blow to the designer's pride but they were potentially devastating to the users.

What the designers failed to realise was that the personal computer is the machine that replaces the pen or typewriter: it is the first part of the second stage. The user still directs the machine, although the energy source is non-human. One has to go through this stage in order to understand the structure and requirements which should be included in the third stage. Unfortunately the main computer manufacturers and DP staff did not take the personal computer seriously – at least, not until IBM came into that sector of the market place.

The personal computer matched the users' needs

In order to understand why the personal computer has proved so effective in the office it is necessary to examine the tasks that are carried out there. These are mostly single user operations – typing a letter, taking information from a file, manipulating financial figures, preparing reports. The personal computer proved to be the ideal machine for such tasks. The software packages help to improve productivity within the office and follow a logical development that can be utilised by the office automation designers for a third stage that works.

The spreadsheet – the first widely used software development tool

Like so many good ideas that have made fortunes for their inventors, the electronic spreadsheet is brilliantly simple in concept. Accountants and others have long used paper spreadsheets – large sheets of paper ruled into rows and columns to give a rectangular array of cells. Each cell can contain a number representing, say, the sales in a given area in a particular month. Certain cells are special and contain totals; for instance, those along the right-hand side might be totals by month, those along the bottom totals by area, with a grand total in the bottom right-hand corner.

Working on paper, you enter the various sales figures in the appropriate places. When they are all entered, you can calculate the various row and column totals. Of course, if any of the figures change you will have to change the totals for both the row and the column in which that cell is located.

The electronic spreadsheet, similarly, has rows, columns and cells in which you can enter sales figures or any other information. The spreadsheet as a whole is much bigger than could be shown on the PC screen, so at any one time you see only a portion of it.

The advantage of the electronic spreadsheet over the paper version is simple: as soon as you enter a value in a cell, or alter the value that was there previously, the row and column totals are automatically recalculated for you. When you see this for the first time, the effect is magical. The uses that the spreadsheet has been put to are vast and in some cases unbelievable – it is little wonder that it is the most widely used software in the office.

The spreadsheet has proved to be a very powerful office automation tool, and the only machine that can run this program cost-effectively is the personal computer. When understanding the three stages in technological development, notice how similar the electronic spreadsheet is to the paper-based stage. There is a natural link between the two stages.

In the development of software tools the stages are likely to progress from the spreadsheet through a range of sophisticated fourth-generation languages. After all the implications have been understood the fifth-generation languages will follow.

It makes sense to use fourth-generation languages before worrying about how to use the fifth-generation. Even so, it is essential to appreciate the developments in this field.

Fifth-generation computing and what it might be able to do

Over the past few years a lot of attention has been paid to expert systems. They have become the 'flavour of the month', the latest buzz word, the great white hope. The only thing they have not become, so far, is used to any great extent.

It is certain that potential mass-market expert-system products are in sight. These will at last bring expert systems to all types of people, not as a toy or a novelty but as something which deserves disk space in the same way, that word-processors, spreadsheets, database management systems and fourth-generation languages deserve disk space.

But first a quick resumé of what an expert system is and what it is supposed to do. An expert system encapsulates human expertise. An expert system running on a computer is the equivalent of a human expert sitting on your desk. This computer expert has the virtues of never making mistakes, never tiring, and never wanting his bills paid. Best of all, you can switch him off when he starts to get boring.

So for a modest outlay it might be possible to have a tax advisor, for instance, sitting in your machine, always able to offer expert tax advice. You will no longer have to waste time contacting a consultant every time you need information about your tax affairs.

Expert systems - how they work

Traditional expert systems are divided into two parts: an *inference engine* and a *knowledge base*. The inference engine is the part of the program that does the 'reasoning', and is able to reason about problems in general. The knowledge base is the material about which it reasons – its area or domain of expertise.

In the case of the hypothetical tax advisor, the inference engine might be software which could equally well reason about a farm's fertiliser requirements, but the knowledge base would contain information specific to the area of tax advice. It is this combination of inference engine and an appropriate knowledge base which makes an expert system expert in a particular field.

The advantages

In theory this arrangement has a number of advantages. The first is that a single well-designed inference engine can be used for many different areas of expertise, provided it is given the appropriate knowledge bases. The second is that, given care in producing the inference engine, the knowledge base can be fairly user-transparent – in other words relatively simple for the naive user to write and understand. That way it becomes apparent just what expertise has been placed in a system, and it becomes very easy to modify and maintain.

An expert system shell

These arguments lead to another idea – that of the expert system shell. This is a program which has an inference engine and a simple means to build up new knowledge bases to run under that inference engine. The Japanese have been to the fore in developing fifth-generation computers associated with expert systems.

The fifth-generation computer

In 1982 the Japanese government's Ministry of Trade and Industry (MITI) began a 10-year project to make the fifth-generation computer. This project is run by the 'Institute for the New Generation Computer Technology' – ICOT for short. The main participants in ICOT are the eight computer manufacturers Fujitsu, Hitachi, NEC, Toshiba, Mitsubishi, Oki, Matsushita and Sharp. They developed a research team in which every member was less than 35 years old at the time they were seconded.

The research laboratory is organised into three sections, one concerned with hardware, one with software, and the other with the rapid development of concrete computer systems as a tool for research purposes.

Research and development plan

The fifth-generation computer research and development project is a ten-year program planned in three phases: an initial phase of three years, an intermediate phase of four years, and a final phase of three years. The initial phase consists of accumulation, evaluation and reorganisation of research results currently available in the field of knowledge and information processing.

In the intermediate phase, the results from the initial phase will be modified, improved and expanded. At the same time efforts will be directed towards combining the individual elements and constructing practical inference subsystems and knowledge base subsystems.

The final phase will focus on the subsystems, improving techniques, reorganisation, and dealing with the details of final objectives.

The computer in the 1990s

The appearance of the fifth-generation computer in the 1990s will not, of course, mean the disappearance of the ordinary computers that are being used now.

It is interesting to forecast the types of computer that will be used in the 1990s. Existing computers will still be used in the field of data processing. Information management, however, will become much more important. Information systems will be constructed at a world level; the latest and most accurate information will be available through a computer network constructed by linking databases from many different places through communication links.

Also, as mentioned previously, there will continue to be a strong demand for computers for numerical computation, and supercomputers performing numerical computation will be used to simulate systems of various kinds. The time is approaching when computer simulation will be used to perform much of the work that is now carried out by pilot plants and various tests using models. Apart from this, an appreciable proportion of the experiments that are carried out in physics and biochemistry will be replaced by computer simulation, and simulation of social phenomena will become common. In the field of engineering, more precise designs will be achieved by using computers.

Apart from such conventional types of computer, new computers for utilising artificial-intelligence techniques will be in use in the 1990s. The main objective of such new computers will be to raise the intellectual capability of humans by assisting intellectual activity in many different ways. For instance, computers will assist in the struggle to achieve a better society. We call such systems 'knowledge information processing systems'. In its narrowest sense, the 'fifth-generation computer' means a computer intended for such knowledge information processing.

Knowledge information processing systems are expected to assist people by performing some of the activities (such as inference and association) required in the processes of decision making. They will also diagnose various systems and act as experts to perform a wide range of human intellectual activities, specifically such work as judgement and design. It is anticipated that such systems will require the ability to understand language and images, and will progressively increase in learning ability. To assist human intellectual activity, they will have to have a man-machine interface that is natural for people. This will mean the ability to exchange information between people and the system using voice or images.

The Fifth Generation Computer Systems (FGCS) project is aimed at promoting the research and development of computer systems for use in the field of knowledge information processing.

Three systems comprising the fifth-generation computers

Basic research is being conducted in Artifical Intelligence (AI), a field that revolves around language understanding. To conduct R&D on a practical level in the field of AI it is necessary to manipulate large amounts of data, and if this data cannot be processed rapidly then the work simply will not be practicable. With today's computers, even simple processing operations require vast amounts of computer power and time. This has proved to be one of the major bottlenecks to furthering practical research work in the field of AI.

Since conventional computers were designed primarily for processing numerical data, they are extremely weak when it comes to processing the non-numerical data so essential to AI. For example, today's computers are extremely limited in their ability to deal with inference functions, and thus association and learning functions.

The development of VLSI technology has brought with it an economical means of enhancing computer hardware functions. It should therefore be possible to improve the hardware functions necessary to process non-numerical data and to perform inference processing. This is one of the goals the FGCS project is striving to achieve. We call this hardware the 'inference processing and problem solving system'.

Even conventional information systems must handle various types of data. This data is retained and utilised in the form of databases. The data stored in databases consists of numeric and character strings. The meaning of this data is understood by the database user, who creates a program based on that understanding in order to obtain the answers he desires.

However, a knowledge information processing system is designed to process knowledge itself. Such a system must store the meanings that data items have in the form of information regarding the mutual inter-relationships between the various data items. It must then use these meanings in carrying out processing. Another of the goals of the Fifth Generation Computer Systems project is to go beyond the processing of 'meaning' and implement a new kind of knowledge base. This will make possible processing that takes into account the environment in which the problem exists. We call this the 'knowledge base system'.

It will be imperative for computers to be easy to operate in order to expand their applications and enable them to be used as tools and/or assistants by large numbers of people.

Ease of operation can be discussed from a number of standpoints. One way of making computers easier to operate is to standardise the way keys are arranged on keyboard input devices. Most programs are input into today's computers by typing them in using standardised keyboards. However, if the computer could be given instructions by *voice* – by talking to it just as we talk to other people – then operating a computer would become a completely natural act.

If humans are to interface with machines in a manner similar to the way humans interface with one other when they exchange information, computers will have to be equipped to understand 'natural' (human) language. Another goal is to realise an intelligent human–machine interface that enables humans to exchange information with machines using voice (speech), pictures and diagrams (graphics) all at the same time. This is called the 'intelligent human–machine interface'.

Chapter Eleven
Information Technology as a Competitive Weapon

The object of using computers is to build and support systems that help knowledge workers to be efficient and effective, and consequently profit the organisation. Information technology is quite rightly viewed in many industries and industrial sectors as a competitive weapon. It is an integral part of any strategic plan. A strategic plan means that management decide what is to be done. There is no pure information system strategy, nor is there any pure financial strategy.

Either a strategy is total or there is no strategy at all. Strategy is based on clear and unambiguous management choices. When management cannot make up its mind on goals, products, systems, competitive position, and a forward plan, there can be no success. The use of information technology is not a substitute for a plan but a means whereby the goal can be achieved – it is a tool, or a weapon.

In many cases, technology *per se* enables newcomers to gain an impressive market share. Technology may not be the most important reason for radical changes in banking, business and industry, but it is a competitive weapon. Information has become the fourth largest resource, after people, material and money.

Banks make millions by making deals more quickly

A professional data communications engineer was hired by a big bank to take charge of installing an international communications network costing more than £1 million. After the job had been completed he was told that the bank had recouped the cost inside 48 hours because of the additional speed at which data could be transmitted. For a bank sending deals around the world, cutting the time from three seconds to two can be very significant.

Expert systems identify deals for dealers

The mass of data now available to each dealer – on which he is required to make split-second decisions – has also thrown up the need for fourth-generation languages and artificial intelligence. Artificial intelligence will be used in the decision support area, predistilling information for the dealer and looking for opportunities. When it comes to arbitrage opportunities, things happen too fast for individual dealers to spot complex cases.

There are likely to be cooperative expert systems for program trading, where a group of dealers decide to make an opportunity happen. Such systems would hold a large number of rules and would monitor fluctuations in the exchange rate or interest rate. When the right combination of factors occurred, the system would prompt the dealer.

Dealers' desks and star wars

Although artificial intelligence skills are not widespread among computer suppliers and tend to be concentrated among the major defence contractors, many financial systems are in fact coming to resemble battlefield command and control systems. It is only a matter of time before they are commonplace in the financial markets. Another big growth area will be in the marketing and sales departments of large organisations, since this area is also one where a vast amount of information has to be analysed and acted upon.

This highlights the need to cope with the increasing pace and importance of information technology. Responsible executives must be able to anticipate, and to respond in a rapid, accurate manner to competitive initiative, in order to identify new opportunities and be able to exploit them. This is the sense of strategic planning. The progression of data processing from batch, closed-shop operations to online interactive implementation with intelligent work-stations on the user's desk has radically changed the way in which business is carried out. It has not only increased users' visibility, but altered the methods of programming the machine. This is the primary reason for the growth in the use of 4GLs, which will in turn lead to expert systems.

Other technological developments

At the same time, technological developments have led to large-scale computer and communications systems. Large systems are not little systems that have outgrown their original size; they are totally different in terms of their design, implementation, verification and maintenance. To achieve integrational technology we must have communication between man and information the way it used to be before the earlier generation of computers broke the link. Both software and hardware must be fully transparent to the user.

The cutting edge of technology accelerates life-cycles

The cutting edge of technology has also accelerated life-cycles. Today we should never project new systems with life-cycles longer than five years. That puts emphasis on cost cutting from the start. The pillars of the new environments are 4GLs and intelligent workstations in the form of the personal computer, as well as communications links between personal computers and the UNIX-based departmental systems and major databases.

Five-year life-cycles also underscore the need to foresee a replacement for the system which may only be in its early design stages. These days it is inadvisable to enter a tunnel until the exit is clear. The point is that falling behind in innovation and modernisation will seriously reduce the competitiveness of any organisation. Financial institutions that do not invest in expert systems will not be successful. The same will go for marketing departments and every other aspect of commerce and business. There is no point in reading about fourth-generation languages and expert systems, you have got to act on your knowledge. As computer and communication technologies march on, even the most automated firm today risks having too many labour-intensive tasks in five years' time. At the same time, five-year life-cycles in information systems investment imply:

(1) Very high and rapid productivity software development.
(2) Development time of less than four months, or at least less than half a year.
(3) Low-cost components (hardware and software) and an open vendor policy.
(4) Support for new functions, previously offered manually or not at all.
(5) Functions already computer-based to be restructured, modernised, personalised and integrated.

Understand the business opportunities that exist

To repeat the advice given above, don't design a new system until you have a notion of the next one. At the same time, make a business opportunity report to focus on the benefit your firm may derive from new systems. Business, industrial and financial institutions, from basic to sophisticated users, emphasise quality as a means of increasing productivity. Improved quality, productivity and effectiveness has become the all-imperative goal.

There are many opportunities to improve personal productivity but the goals are changing. Until recently improved office productivity focused primarily on the secretary and the clerical worker. Now attention has turned to the productivity and performance of managers and knowledge workers. Information is both the input and the output of knowledge workers. As the business world becomes more complex, it generates and uses more information. This state of affairs results in a number of situations. It:

- causes office bottlenecks
- diverts management from important actions, and
- hampers productivity.

One of the knowledge worker's most powerful tools is effective control over the proliferation of paper-based information. Interactive solutions, personal workstations, personal files, and corporate-wide communications find much of their justification in this effective information control. Productivity improves; the three most important dimensions are completeness, power and simplicity. Simplicity comprises both of ease of learning and ease of use, and it in turn is heavily affected by integration.

Integration means ease of moving among the various functions of a product, and making different components appear similar to the user. This is normally achieved by using identical subroutines and common files. For integrity, security, and cost reasons, however, the appropriate tools have to be carefully tailored to the users' requirements. They must be embedded in a total information management concept. Corporate information plans should answer the following six questions in a factual and documented manner.

1. **Where are we now?**

2. **Why change?**

3. **What can be done?**

4. **What could we do?**

5. **How do we get there?**

6. **Did we get there?**

Fig. 11.1 Questions every business should ask.

(1) **Where are we now?**
This calls for an assessment of current resources, strengths and weaknesses.
(2) **Why change?**
To exploit new opportunities we should identify business perspectives, market evolutions and technical developments. To survive, we should position our own company in line with the forces of the future.
(3) **What can be done?**
A strategic aftermath, obstacles, risks, opportunities, findings, and cost benefits are part of the answer to be given to this question.
(4) **What could we do?**
We must make basic choices, evaluate components, analyse policy decisions, proceed with system integration and elaborate possible implementation strategies.
(5) **How do we get there?**
To answer this question we must consider client relationships, product evolution, resource allocations, business systems development, management information projects, project management priorities and training.
(6) **Did we get there?**
That is the feedback. We need to be able to focus on the proper corrective action and to obtain it we must have matrix measurements and appraisal.

Manage information as a product

Above all, we must be managing information as a product. In most financial and industrial organisations, information is not managed. It is available in overabundance or not at all. It is seldom timely and complete. And it is provided at a cost that cannot be determined. Quite often today's approach to information management is based on yesterday's concepts and technologies. The image of what can be done with modern media dates back three or four decades. Yet every six months something very significant happens and changes the way in which we look at our workplace. As well as we can currently project, this will continue to be true in some measure well into the 1990s.

When new technologies are available to automate work which was previously manual, and are proved to be very effective, organisations resist them rather than embrace them. There are many reasons for their reluctance to put computer-based software technology into practice. One is their lack of perception of the penalties from obsolescence (low product quality and higher labour costs), and the return on investment in software tools is not well understood. Even among businesses known to be sharp and cost-cutting there is ignorance about accounting practice for software assets. There is also reluctance to engage in continued education, training and information distribution to keep programmers and users aware of the new technologies.

To level the balance a comparative evaluation of competing technologies must be performed. This is not possible without full-scale experiments in realistic environments. Then, once the choice is identified, the actual introduction into practice must be organised, personnel trained, and programs that were constructed in the old way adapted to the new technology. This underscores the importance of technology transfer.

Technology transfer always takes place between two organisations; one is the *source* and the other is the *recipient*. The secret of successful transfer is to find the best match of peers. A specific information technology mission should be to analyse issues in the medium to long term (2–5 years) that are of strategic importance to the organisation. Software development has become such an issue, and it will be an even greater issue in the future.

Critical questions to ask

The critical question to ask is 'What support technologies are necessary: telecommunication networks, PC software, databases, or user facilities?' The next question is how your company organises itself to capitalise on these technical resource capabilities and the opportunities that present themselves.

The cost and value associated with technology transfer should be objectively evaluated and an implementation plan established thereafter. Control action should include management authorisation, design, review, budgeting, timetabling, quality-control and insurance. These are practical subjects with a major impact on the value-added structure of the business. Strategic issues in technological transfer itself call for interdisciplinary analyses. A corporate rather than departmental focus is required for successful resolution.

Innovation brings problems

Innovation, however, brings problems and headaches in its wake. As an obvious illustration, publishing was forced to develop a new framework for discussion of such issues as intellectual copyright. Questions relating to data protection, computer piracy, transborder data flows, copyright, and public and private sector interaction are no longer just professional problems, but matters of national and international governmental concern.

What do we mean when we speak of information as a resource?

- Something of fundamental value like money, capital goods, labour or raw materials.

- Something with specific and measurable characteristics such as a method of collection, utilities and uses.
- Input which can be transformed into useful output.
- Something that can be capitalised.
- Something that presents top management with a variety of development choices.

People do not know their future information needs

Commonly, people do not know what information they need until a particular set of circumstances arise; then they want very specific information immediately. This state of affairs has resulted in people hoarding information and data on the off-chance that they will need some of it. The 80/20 rule applies – 20% of the information will satisfy 80% of the demands. The problem is that no one knows which part is the vital 20%.

As a result information overload is common in large organisations. Ever since the advent of photocopiers, people have tended to make extra copies just in case someone might like one. A major multinational survey on duplicated paper discovered that 40 copies were made of each piece of paper of which 15 were kept indefinitely. Most organisations suffer from paper proliferation and it is often made worse by massive computer reports. What has to be understood is the true cost, not just the cost of producing, filing, storing and retrieving information but the cost of people's time.

People gain status or recognition within an organisation as a direct result of their knowledge and their information resources. Quite naturally, they guard that information jealously. They are reluctant to share it with others for fear of personal loss and tend to surround their knowledge with mystique and folklore. The individual thus creates an image of being indispensable, and maintains the status quo.

Fourth-generation languages will simplify the information game.

Part 2. DOS, UNIX, DBMS and 4GLs

Chapter Twelve
DOS and UNIX Features

DOS has become the de facto operating system standard for single-user microcomputers, and UNIX is clearly heading for the same title in the multi-user arena. The importance of both these operating systems in today's and tomorrow's computing makes it worthwhile to take a detailed look at the main features of both and their relevance to the fourth-generation environment. We look at DOS briefly (those that require a full coverage on DOS are referred to the many excellent texts available). This is followed by a study of UNIX features with particular reference to databases, fourth-generation languages and the future convergence of both these operating systems.

DOS file structure

DOS is predominantly concerned with organising and maintaining file details on disks (both floppy and hard disk). The name 'Disk Operating System' says it all. The history of DOS shows that it was not developed as a sophisticated operating system, but rather as a functional one that could serve a user's needs simply in single-user mode.

A floppy disk or hard disk is looked upon by DOS as being divided into a number of 'clusters'. Every file occupies a number of clusters, though under normal disk usage a newly-created file is unlikely to occupy a contiguous area of storage. Once a user has created files, then operations such as deletion of files or changing their size will cause unused clusters to be scattered throughout the disk. Files are used dynamically, so as long as there are sufficient unused clusters, new files can always be created.

All files are treated by DOS as a stream of bytes. DOS uses two special areas on disk to keep track of where files are residing – the *file allocation table* (FAT) and the *directory*. The FAT has an entry for every cluster on the storage unit. If a cluster is allocated to a fragmented file then the FAT entry will have a pointer to the next cluster, which in turn will have a pointer to the next cluster, and so on. This ensures that having found one cluster of a file, DOS can always find the next one.

The directory has an entry for every file, giving its name, its size in bytes, the date and time of last modification and other information. It also has a pointer to the FAT entry for the first cluster of a file, thus allowing all clusters making up a file to be accessed. The directory has a fixed length, limiting the number of files that can be stored. However, it is possible to create sub-directories, which in turn can have sub-directories, and so on, so that the number of files that can be stored is only limited by the physical storage space available. The top-level directory is termed the *root directory*. The benefit of sub-directories comes to the fore when using a hard disk. Once a user has access to a hard disk it will quickly become cluttered with very large numbers of files, until it becomes very difficult to remember what they are used for. Sub-directories help to group files relating to the same subject together so that access to them is easier. Sub-directories also make it possible to have files with the same name (but different contents) in different directories.

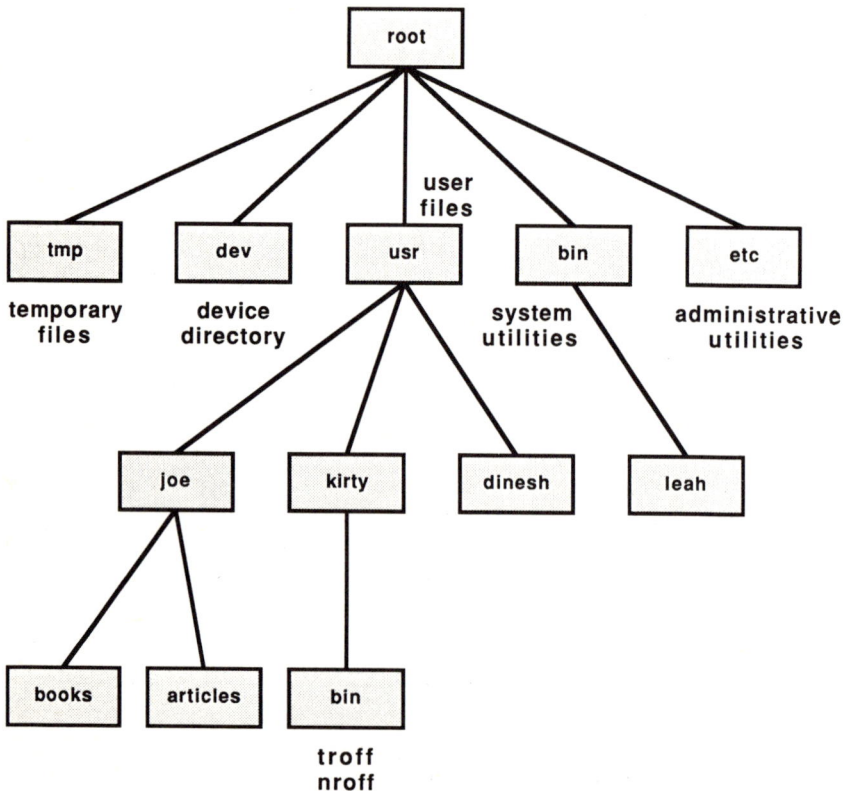

Fig. 12.1 A simple UNIX filesystem structure.

DOS features

The *command interpreter* is the part of DOS that translates the command language that the user employs to communicate with DOS. Whenever the user is not running a program, DOS is waiting for a command to be entered and to act upon it. The user can ascertain that DOS is waiting by looking for the system prompt. Some of the basic commands available include:

- **MD, CD** and **RD**: respectively 'Make Directory', 'Change Directory' and 'Remove Directory'. For example, typing:

  C>md dinesh

  from the root directory (assuming the active drive is the hard disk) will create a sub-directory called 'dinesh'.
- **PROMPT**: allows a customised system prompt, which is particulary useful when using sub-directories. For example:

  prompt $p $g

  will display the root directory system prompt as:

  C:\ >

  Moving from the root directory to the sub-directory 'dinesh' by issuing the command

  C:\ >cd dinesh

  will change the system prompt to:

  C:\dinesh >
- **DIR**: displays the name and other details of files in the current directory. Typing

  C:\dinesh >dir/p

  will display the information a page at a time.
- **COPY**: to copy a file to another disk or another directory. For example:

  C:\ >copy \dinesh\mytext.doc \joe\histext.doc

  issued from the root directory will copy the file 'mytext.doc' in the sub-directory 'dinesh' to the new file 'histext.doc' in the sub-directory 'joe'. If the current operational directory is 'dinesh' then

  C:\dinesh >copy mytext.doc \joe\histext.doc

  will copy 'mytext.doc' to the new file 'histext.doc' in the sub-directory 'joe'. Note that the 'copied to' filename 'histext.doc' could have been kept the

same as the 'copied from' filename, i.e. 'mytext.doc'.
- **DEL**: to delete a file. For example:

    C:\dinesh >del *.*

will erase all files in the 'dinesh' directory. The 'del' command has to be used with great care. Wildcard conventions are allowed for the majority of commands so that

    C:\dinesh >del din*.doc

will erase all files in the current directory that begin with the letters 'din' and have a file extension of 'doc'.
- **TYPE**: to display the contents of a file on the screen.

Batch files and the AUTOEXEC.BAT file

When the user wants to run a program he types the name of the program to be executed in response to the system prompt. If, for example, the following is issued at the system prompt in the 'dinesh' sub-directory:

    C:\dinesh >dinprog

then DOS will search for a file called 'dinprog.com', 'dinprog.exe' or 'dinprog.bat'. The first two are 'program files' and the difference between them need not concern us. The last one, with the 'bat' extension is called a *batch file* and has precedence in the order of execution over the program files. A batch file essentially contains a sequence of DOS commands, just as they would be entered at the keyboard. The main idea of batch files is to save the user from re-keying the same set of commands every time a particular task is to be done. As an example, consider the following simple batch file called 'mybatch.bat':

```
del *.bak
ws
dir *.doc
```

To execute this batch file (in the sub-directory 'dinesh'), simply type the batch filename:

    C:\dinesh >mybatch

This will cause the computer to:

- delete all files with an extension of 'bak'
- execute the program 'ws' (which is in fact the word-processing package WordStar) and
- on exiting WordStar, display the names of all files with an extension 'doc'.

The DOS Batch Language also allows for conditional statements within the batch file so that control can be provided over the execution of the process.

The AUTOEXEC.BAT file is a special batch file. If it exists on the default drive when the computer is switched on or rebooted, it will be executed automatically. As an example, consider the contents of the following AUTOEXEC.BAT file:

```
ver
prompt $p $g
date
time
lotus
```

This will cause the computer to:

- display the version of the DOS operating system
- set the system prompt to the required format
- ask for the date and time to be set
- execute the Lotus 123 spreadsheet access program and
- on leaving Lotus 123, return to the system prompt.

Such batch files are highly worthwhile for those users who only employ a computer for a single task, or for setting up parameters for the customised execution of a program.

Filters

Filters are programs that perform a specified function on an input file and pass the results to an output file. For example:

- **SORT:** sorts files into alphabetical or numerical order.
- **FIND:** searches for a specified pattern of characters in a file.
- **MORE:** displays the contents of a file a page at a time.

Redirection and pipes

All input and output devices are treated by DOS as a file, so programs have a *main input file* (the keyboard, for example) and a *main output file* (e.g. the screen). Redirection allows the input or output file to be a named disk file or a physical device. For example:

```
C:\dinesh >type mytext.doc
```

will cause the contents of the file 'mytext.doc' to be displayed on the screen;

```
C:\dinesh >type mytext.doc > yourtext.doc
```

will send the output to the new file 'yourtext.doc' instead of the screen, and

C:\dinesh >type mytext.doc > prn

will send the output to the printer.

A *pipe* is a mechanism by which the output of one program becomes the input of another. For example:

C:\dinesh >type mytext.doc | sort > mysorted.doc

will send the contents of 'mytext.doc' to the DOS filter 'sort'. This will sort it (parameters are usually needed to determine the type of sorting required) and pass it in sorted form to the new file 'mysorted.doc'. Complex processes may be set up using redirection and pipes. DOS features such as filters, redirection and pipes are ideas borrowed from the UNIX operating system.

DOS 3.1 and onwards

DOS 3.1 and onwards has a number of new features, especially for addressing PCs in a local area network. The main network features include:

- The sharing of files by setting 'read', 'write', or 'read/write' access permissions, and denying access to other users while the file is being used.
- The ability to 'lock' a range of bytes within a file, so that record locking can be implemented by application programs.

Also available with DOS 3.1 are the Microsoft Net Core Protocols (NCP) and NETBIOS. The NCPs are a set of network utilities designed to be independent of network hardware, and include the Redirector program, which reroutes workstation requests to another computer on the network using the NCP. NETBIOS (Network Basic Input/Output System) is the network equivalent of BIOS, and incorporates a series of low-level sub-routines that enable applications developed to this interface to run on any NETBIOS compatible network. NETBIOS has been incorporated into a number of different local area network systems, including the IBM Token Ring and AT&T's Starlan.

Restrictions of DOS

One of DOS's main drawbacks has been its limitation of allowing applications only 640K of memory to work in. This limit is hindering the further development of sophisticated applications. Many database management systems and 4GLs running under DOS would benefit from the availability of greater memory, rather than employing program management techniques to cope with the limited memory. These techniques usually have an adverse effect on application performance. To combat the problem, Lotus Corporation and Intel got together to produce a memory expansion board (called the Above Board) that allows Lotus 123 applications to address more than the 640K limit (up to an additional 2Mb of memory). However, even though the protocol specifications of the board are available to software developers, it has not been widely adopted.

Bill Gates, chairman of Microsoft, has said that 'the evolution of DOS won't allow the development of tomorrow's applications. Software developers are hitting the 640K limit already with single applications.' It is interesting to note that the original DOS 1.0 for the 8088 chip took 15 programmers four months to develop. The next version of DOS (ie OS/2) for the 80286 chip has 180 programmers working on it and is still more than a year away from completion.

It is not commonly known that Microsoft, producers of the largest selling single-user operating system (MS-DOS), also have nearly 200,000 installations of their UNIX-based operating system Xenix on PCs. To take further advantage of this, Microsoft have entered into a technology transfer agreement with AT&T to jointly develop and market a version of UNIX for 80386 chip-based PCs. In the end it will be software developers who will decide which multi-tasking, multi-user operating system to bank on for the new generation of 32-bit processors. UNIX seems the prime candidate.

UNIX

UNIX is a multi-tasking, multi-user, time-sharing operating system. It allocates the resources of the computer between a number of processes running concurrently. The key elements of the UNIX operating system are:

- The kernel
- The file system
- The shell command interpreter and language
- Development tools and applications.

The kernel

The *kernel* is the heart of the UNIX operating system and represents about 5% of the system software. The kernel is the only part of the operating system permanently resident in memory and on which the system relies. It looks after the processor, allocation of memory, the filestore and the communications between the program and the kernel via system calls. The kernel is also responsible for scheduling tasks, which is done on a time-sharing basis. Each process is allocated a time-slice which can be of varying duration – processes with the longest time-slice have a higher priority. The kernel also controls file management, including the 'fork' system call, which creates a duplicate of any file before processing.

The multi-tasking facility allows a user to run a number of processes at the same time from the same terminal. The main process in use will run in the foreground. All other processes will run in the background, normally at a lower priority. Multi-tasking is ideal for work that:

- involves no operator intervention
- may be lengthy and time-consuming
- has a low completion priority.

To set a task running in the background simply type the command followed by an '&'. Restrictions to multi-tasking are:

- A process running in background mode cannot accept input from the keyboard.
- The more processes that are run at the same time, the slower the machine will appear to carry out tasks.

The shell

The *shell* is the user interface of the UNIX system and is run every time a user logs onto the system. The shell is independent of the kernel, which it surrounds. Conceptually, the shell is just another program for the kernel. It receives its arguments (from the command line) in the same way as any other program. This means that a UNIX system can have a number of different shells, and it does.

There are two main shells available to the UNIX user: the AT&T shell ('sh') written by Steve Bourne and referred to as the Bourne Shell, and the C-Shell ('csh') from the University of California at Berkeley. The C-Shell is popular among the programming community because of its C-language-like syntax. The main functions of a shell program include:

- filename expansion
- command substitution
- redirection and piping of input and output
- invoking programs with filenames and arguments.

The shell is also a structured programming language, very much on the lines of the Job Control Language found in other operating systems; it allows the creation of files of commands with full control of the flow of operations. These command files are termed *shell scripts*. The language allows the sequencing and combining of all UNIX utilities and application programs into a single script, which can be invoked by a single command. The shell enables users to enhance and build on UNIX system capabilities, and to adapt the operating system to many user operations without using a compiler or link editor.

The C language and a bit of UNIX philosphy

The UNIX operating system and the C language are effectively synonymous with each other, and closely interrelated. UNIX was originally written, like all other operating systems of the time, in assembly language. This was and still is a lengthy and error-prone process. Ken Thompson and Dennis Ritchie (also of Bell Laboratories) decided to do to computer languages what UNIX did to operating systems; develop a powerful but succinct portable computer language. BCPL (Basic Combined Programming Language) was the starting point. Thompson stripped BCPL down to its basic features and the resulting interpreted language was named simply B. Ritchie then took the best parts of B and reworked them until he had a fast compiled language that provided data structures. He named this simple and elegant language C. It was felt that it was best suited for use as a systems language, allowing programmers to express concepts clearly without being tied to any particular hardware. At the same time it was efficient enough to avoid the need for assembly language to gain extra speed. The compactness of C, with only 30 reserved words, and the provision of libraries for standard input/output functions, meant that the task of porting C onto other hardware architectures was considerably reduced and simplified.

In 1973 UNIX itself was rewritten in C by Ritchie. First, all code not specific to a particular hardware architecture was taken out and re-written, to aid portability. Next, various utilities were added. Finally the kernel itself was rewritten in C, leaving only those parts that were machine dependent to be coded in assembly language (about 5% of the total code). This change from assembly language into C had the added benefit of making the development version of UNIX easier to debug and maintain.

The C version of UNIX encourages the developer

The C version of UNIX permits and encourages the developer to write small programs, each with a limited and clearly defined function, and to have them linked together, running concurrently if need be, through the mechanism of pipes and redirection. UNIX was developed to build a comfortable relationship with the machine, and to explore new ideas and inventions in operating systems and other software. This approach to system development led to the two well-known UNIX maxims:

- Make each program do one thing well. To do a new job, build afresh rather than complicate old programs by adding new features.
- Expect the output of every program to become the input to another program. Don't clutter output with extraneous information.

An operating system with such a pedigree would not, under normal circumstances, stand much of a chance as a viable commercial operating system. However, it has succeeded as such, and the first commercial release of UNIX from AT&T in 1979 opened the way for the commercial exploitation of UNIX.

It also was the spur for developers to add various languages and development tools.

Development tools and applications

The outermost layer of UNIX contains development tools and applications. A typical UNIX system will come with a C compiler, assembler, syntax and portability checker ('lint'). The 'make' tool controls related groups of computer programs. The Source Code Control System ('sccs') keeps track of succeeding versions of a piece of software. A file comparator ('diff') shows the exact differences between two text files. A lexical analyser ('lex') is available, so is 'awk', which searches for patterns in a text and performs actions on lines that include the pattern.

Also available are text editing facilities such as 'nroff' for text formatting, 'troff' for photo-typesetting, and 'ed' and 'vi' for text creation. The list is almost endless. The power of UNIX is in its ability to help the developer use existing tools and employ them to build even more powerful ones.

The tools available can be split up into different sections, and include:

- **System Administration:** a set of tools for the day-to-day housekeeping of the UNIX system.
- **Directory and File Management:** a set of tools to reduce directory and file manipulation operations (which normally consist of multiple steps) to single-step operations.
- **Help Utilities:** to provide an interactive menu-driven help facility giving information on the UNIX system.
- **Inter-Process Communication:** a set of tools to allow inter-process communication with the UNIX inter-process communication facilities, by way of messages, semaphores and shared memory. These tools provide for two-way communication among UNIX system processes.

Others include tools for:
- line printer spooler management
- system performance measurement
- document spell checking and
- graphics.

The UNIX file structure

UNIX has no internal file structure associated with the notion of records within a file or fields within a record. In UNIX every file is a stream of bytes, whether it contains text, program source code, executable object code or the disk directory. Application programs usually demand a structure in their data files, but UNIX does not enforce any constraints. Applications are thus allowed to create their own data file structure.

Directories and their organisation

UNIX files are organised as a hierarchy of directories and sub-directories. Such a directory structure allows users to organise the filing system to fit their specific requirements and to keep files in logically related groups. The top-level directory is called the 'root' directory and contains the executable kernel of UNIX in binary form, as well as links to a number of important directories including:

- **\bin,** where system utilities and executable files are found.
- **\dev,** the device directory.
- **\etc,** where administrative programs and data files are kept.
- **\usr,** the directory where all user files are stored.
- **\tmp,** a place where temporary files can be created as and when needed.

Directories are treated as files, so there is no limit to the number of directory entries. In fact the directories do not contain files; they hold pointers or 'links' with which the system can locate the actual data. Thus a directory is a file containing the link information, called the *i-node*.

i-node

Each physical file on the system has an associated i-node, which provides the system with a description of the file and contains information on the following:

- the owner of the file
- the group owner identification
- file type (regular, directory or special)
- file size
- file protection information
- number of links
- date of creation
- date of most recent access and modification
- pointers to the data blocks.

Special device directory

All physical devices (terminals, memory, storage units, printers, etc.)

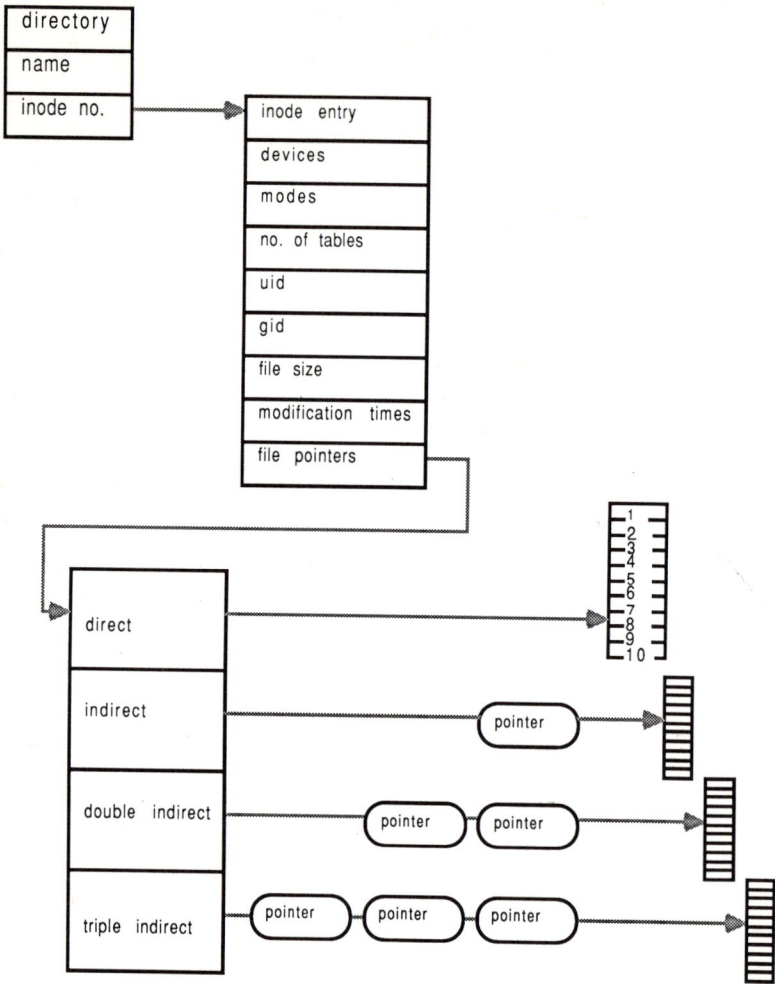

Fig. 12.2 UNIX i-node table structure.

supported by the system appear, like files, as entries in the /dev directory. These devices are accessed by users and programs as if they were actually files. A user may treat devices as files, but the UNIX systems programmer must write device-drivers for these devices so that communication with the system is possible. The operating system has to access the devices through the device-drivers, so devices are also known as *special files*.

Special files can be either *character-oriented* (for devices such as terminals, modems and printers) or *block-oriented* (for devices such as memory and storage units) in which case they transfer data in fixed unit blocks of 512K or more.

File security
The UNIX file system provides protection on each file at three levels and for three categories of user. Each file has three permission attributes: *read*, *write* and *execute*. For each type of user, the three permission attributes apply. The types of users are: *user* (owner of the file), *group* (people in the same group as the owner) and *other* (everybody else). The careful combination of these permissions can lead to very secure systems, which is of the utmost importance for commercial applications within a database and fourth-generation environment.

Dynamic file allocation
On creation of a file, UNIX, unlike certain other operating systems, does not ask for the length of the file in advance. A UNIX file just keeps on growing. Writing the first item of data to a newly created file allocates the first block of storage found in the free block table. When another block is required, the next free block is allocated. When a file is deleted, or its size is reduced, blocks are set free and returned to the free block table.

Fragmentation
The continual growth of a file will, under normal circumstances, lead to data fragmentation on the storage device. UNIX deals with fragmentation in a very simple way. Disk space is allocated to a file in blocks, and the contents table in the i-node cannot accommodate more than ten block addresses. The eleventh entry in the contents table is the address of a further table of data block addresses. To gain access to this, an 'indirect' addressing technique has to be employed. In this second table of data block addresses the eleventh entry again contains the address of a further table, the third table of data block addresses.

If files approach their theoretical maximum size (the maximum file size is determined by the 'file size' field in the i-node, which allows the limit on a file to be 4 gigabytes), then a large proportion of the data is only accessible by 'triple-indirect' addressing. In other words, to access a piece of data on storage, the system has to access three separate tables to get the data addresses.

The UNIX file system was designed and optimised to handle small files only, since the original use was for program development and text processing. The file system as it stands is not designed to handle very large databases. This limitation is overcome by the use of a *raw disk*, which we cover later in this chapter.

Redirection and pipes

Each process in UNIX triggers the opening of three files:

- The *standard input* ('stdin').
- The *standard output* ('stdout').
- The *standard error output* ('stderr').

Redirection allows any process to obtain its input from a file or device. For example typing

ls > /dev/lp

at the system prompt will send the list of files in the current directory to the system printer rather than the screen. The input to a program can be controlled in a similar manner.

A *filter* is a program that accepts standard input, manipulates and processes the information it reads, then writes the result to its standard output. This is a very simple idea but has powerful implications when used in conjunction with *pipes*. A pipe connects two programs to form a data pipeline. All programs in a pipeline run simultaneously. As soon as the first program has put a whole block (512K) into the pipe, the next program will start up. Programs further down the line get their input in dribs and drabs as the preceding programs produce output. For example, typing:

ls : wc

will send the output of 'ls' (the list of files in the current directory) into 'wc' (a program that counts the number of words in a file) to give the number of files in the directory. Further,

ls -d : sort : lpr

will take the output of 'ls' (the '-d' is an optional parameter informing the system that only a list of the directories is required), sort it and then spool it for printing on the line printer.

File and record locking

A crucial consideration for operating systems in a commercial environment is that of simultaneous access or update by more than one user to a file or parts of a file. Locking is standard with UNIX System V Release 2.0 onwards. As mentioned earlier the UNIX file system has no notion of records or fields, and thus UNIX locking is performed at a byte level. The application program or database management system must decide what area is to be locked – a record, groups of records, a field, groups of fields or even a single byte. Unfortunately UNIX only provides for 'exclusive' locks; once a file area is locked no other process can access that same area. This situation is usually not satisfactory for commercial databases, where a 'shared' lock is the norm.

In a shared lock, if an area of the file is locked it does not stop other processes from reading the data, only from writing to it.

Buffering and the 'sync' call

Disk input and output is buffered in UNIX. The UNIX kernel organises and manages a pool of buffers corresponding to disk blocks. A process performing a write operation on a data file on disk does not access the disk directly but updates the contents of the appropriate buffer. If this buffer has to be released to make room for new data being read in, the kernel writes it back to disk. Otherwise, physical writing occurs as a result of the 'sync' system call. UNIX has a background process running continuously and issuing the sync call every thirty seconds, causing all buffers to be flushed to disk. The problems associated with this procedure for applications, in particular database systems, are:

- An application program does not know whether a physical update has taken place or not.
- An application program has no control over when an update takes place.
- Physical updates do not necessarily occur in the order the application might expect.

These problems are major concerns in the event of a hardware failure, because there is a high likelihood that important data will not have been physically written to disk since the modification was made. A database can thus be left in an indeterminate state. The solution is to write one's own file system and use the 'raw' disk.

Raw disk

The UNIX file system can be bypassed by directly reading from and writing to the 'raw' disk. In essence this involves treating a disk partition as a device rather than a structured file system. Most database management systems and 4GLs support a raw disk facility to overcome UNIX's sometimes cumbersome file system. The advantages of using the raw disk include:

- Faster access to data in storage.
- File fragmentation can be minimised by optimising the file organisation.
- UNIX buffering can be avoided.
- Customised directory structures can be implemented to provide greater security and permission access.
- Logical files do not have to reside within a single file system, and can be spread over multiple disk volumes.

Mountable storage

The 'root' directory of the file system always resides on the same physical device, is kept on the hard disk, and has to be present when the system is booted up. However, it is not necessary for the entire file system to be confined to this one device. Any other storage device (disk or tape) can be 'mounted' onto any directory in the current file system. The effect of mounting a filestore volume onto a file is to transform all references to that directory into a reference to the root directory of the mounted file system. After the mount there is virtually no distinction between files on the removable media and those on the permanent file system. Files are accessed in the same way as files from the root file system. The only limitations are that a file cannot be linked or renamed across file systems. Renaming involves changing the filename from one directory to another; it does not physically move the file, only the directory entry. If renaming were allowed across file systems, then it would be possible to create a directory pointer to, say, an empty diskette drive, or worse, to a diskette drive which contained another floppy. Filestores may be mounted and unmounted while UNIX is running, and without any interruptions to the service.

The Super User

There is a special user in a UNIX environment called the Super User or System Administrator. The Super User manages the system resources and generally oversees the way the system is used. The Super User has the ability to bypass all protections on the system to:

- Create and remove users
- Manage passwords and password aging
- Manage user groups
- Add terminals, printers and other devices to the system
- Make regular backups of the data
- Process system accounts data
- Monitor security breaches
- Help users.

Passwords and security

Since UNIX is a multi-user system, there is more to starting a session than just switching the machine on. In practice it will most likely already be on, and UNIX will be up and running; not just awaiting a command to be issued from the user, but doing its housekeeping. To employ UNIX services the user has to log on, that is identify himself to the system. The user will not be let into the system unless he has been set up as an authorised user and has a password. The password is not echoed onto the screen. User passwords are kept in an encrypted form within the system and are very resistant to tampering. Information about user logins is contained in a password file, where each record contains details about a particular user. The details held include:

- login name
- encrypted password
- user identification number
- group identification number
- user comments
- user's home directory
- the login program (usually the shell).

Communications

Though UNIX is a development of the Bell Laboratories stable, until recently it was not very polished in the area of communications facilities. The UNIX utility 'uucp' (UNIX to UNIX communications package) provides for an error-checking file transfer facility between UNIX machines. A user will request uucp for a file transfer, and UNIX will transfer the file when it can.

Another method uses the 'cu' (call UNIX) facility, whereby a user can log onto another UNIX machine via its login port (terminal port).

The latest version of UNIX (System V Release 3.0) has a number of additional facilities, notably the implementation of the Streams Input/Output system, which was first proposed by Dennis Ritchie (co-developer with Ken Thompson of the C language) in 1984. It also includes the distributed file system RFS (Remote File System).

AT&T UNIX System V Release 3.0

The latest release of UNIX addresses a number of criticisms that have been made about UNIX's viability as a commercial operating system. The most important of these are:

- **Demand Paging.** Release 2.0 of UNIX performed memory management by using a 'swapping' mechanism, whereby an entire program had to be read into memory before it could be executed. Release 3.0 offers *demand paging* using virtual memory techniques, where a process is defined as a set of 2K 'pages' that are loaded into memory one by one when referenced. The major benefit of demand paging is that it reduces the time spent swapping programs in and out, especially when the system may not be configured with the maximum memory. Also, by extension, it will allow programs to run that are physically larger than the memory in the computer.

- **Shared Libraries.** A shared library is a set of routines that is accessible dynamically at run-time rather than being combined with each application program at 'load-time'. This means that the application will occupy less physical disk storage and less space in memory.

- **Mandatory Locking.** Release 2.0 of UNIX only provided for 'advisory' locking (or 'exclusive' locks), where locks are only effective if all processes use similar locking strategies. This means that it is possible for a process to ignore locks and read/write a locked file. In Release 3.0 both 'advisory' and 'mandatory' locking is available at the file and record level. Mandatory locking provides the facility to stop any process reading/writing a file or record without permission. Furthermore, UNIX will not allow a file to be overwritten if the file has been mandatorily locked.

- **Streams.** 'Streams' is the most important enhancement to UNIX since the original concept. It is a modular approach to input and output, which allows specific communication protocols to be removed from device drivers and placed in the kernel, each with a standard interface to the stream facility. It is a general set of tools for the development of communication and networking services within the UNIX environment.

- **Remote File System.** The Remote File System is implemented using Streams, which makes it independent of any particular network protocol (hardware or software). Eventually Streams will be a general facility for sending data through the kernel by using pipes, and it will give third parties the opportunity to develop network components such as the OSI modules. RFS provides transparent access between local and remote UNIX file systems, keeping track of file accesses and automatically providing file and record locking.

Same software available under DOS and UNIX

DOS is now established as the standard for single-user PCs. UNIX leads the way to satisfying the needs of a multi-tasking, multi-user operating system. The number of applications available for the DOS environment far exceeds that of any other operating system. In the field of database management systems, UNIX has led the way as the development vehicle. These UNIX applications are also being ported into the DOS environment, to take advantage of the large number of PC users. In the opposite direction, PC software producers are porting their software onto UNIX, to take advantage of the multi-user marketplace. This crossing of applications from DOS to UNIX or vice versa has been made commercially viable by having the original application written in the C language. Though COBOL versions are available under both DOS and UNIX, they have had minimal success in this area.

C compilers are available under DOS, and under UNIX it is the software development language. So applications using C under either DOS or UNIX have a comfortable transition from one environment to another. The associated cost is far less than that of rewriting the software.

DOS and UNIX converge

The close similarity between the DOS and UNIX file structures and the importance of both DOS and UNIX can be gauged from the number of products available which allow a PC and a UNIX machine to work together. The most widely available is the PC Interface package. PC Interface allows a number of PCs to be physically connected into a UNIX host. The user benefits by running local PC applications with the facilities of a multi-user operating system. From the DOS environment, the power of UNIX can be accessed through familiar DOS commands while sharing the UNIX hard disk with other UNIX or PC Interface users. UNIX facilities such as print spooling and file security are all available to the PC user from within the DOS environment. The three major components of the package are:

- PC Interface.
- Terminal emulation.
- Context switch.

PC Interface

This part of the package allows the UNIX host to be used as a shared resource between DOS users. DOS files may be retrieved, manipulated and stored on the UNIX hard disk in DOS format and, if need be, translated into UNIX format using translation utilities. From the PC environment the remote hard disk appears as a named drive (either C: if a floppy based machine, or D: if hard disk based). So, for example, the copying of files between the remote hard disk and the local storage can be achieved in the normal way by using the copy command.

The utilities available for manipulating UNIX files from DOS are:

- **DOS2UNIX** and **UNIX2DOS:** allows for file format conversion from UNIX to DOS or vice versa
- **LOCKS:** allows locks to be set on a DOS file on the UNIX host, so that other users do not access it when it is being used
- **UCHMOD:** allows the alteration of access permissions of DOS files on the UNIX host, preventing unauthorised access by other PC or UNIX users
- **UDIR:** produces a UNIX-like directory listing of DOS files on the UNIX host
- **UREN:** allows for renaming of files
- **PRINTER:** the options 'local' or 'remote' will cause any printing to be sent either to the printer attached to the PC or the default UNIX host printer respectively.

Terminal emulation

The terminal emulation software allows the PC to act as terminal to the UNIX machine. In addition the following facilities are available:

• sending, receiving and storing files from the UNIX host
• listing the contents of a DOS file while connected to the UNIX host.

Context switch

The Context switch enables the PC user to switch back and forth between the DOS and UNIX environments. For example, a DOS application can be frozen at any time by the user, who may then switch into terminal emulation mode to the UNIX host. The reverse also holds: a UNIX process may be 'switched out of' and frozen while the user picks up where he left off in the DOS application.

IBM, AIX and UNIX

In early 1985 IBM introduced the 6150 computer system (called the RT PC in the USA). It runs an IBM implementation of UNIX called AIX (Advanced Interactive eXecutive) based on AT&T UNIX System V, with additional features from the Berkeley 4.2 UNIX.

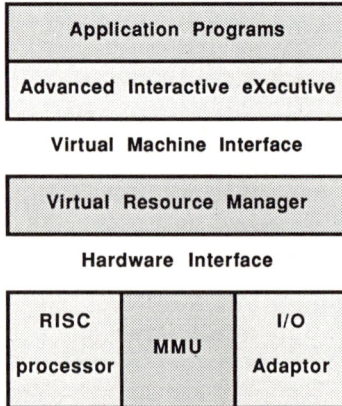

```
┌─────────────────────────────────────┐
│       Application  Programs          │
├─────────────────────────────────────┤
│   Advanced  Interactive  eXecutive   │
└─────────────────────────────────────┘
        Virtual  Machine  Interface

┌─────────────────────────────────────┐
│      Virtual  Resource  Manager      │
└─────────────────────────────────────┘
          Hardware  Interface

┌──────────┬─────────┬────────┐
│   RISC   │         │  I/O   │
│          │   MMU   │        │
│ processor│         │ Adaptor│
└──────────┴─────────┴────────┘
```

Fig. 12.3   IBM 6150/AIX architecture.

The processor is a full 32-bit microprocessor based on Reduced Instruction Set Computer (RISC) technology. In essence, RISC technology says that 'more can be done with less', where the less refers to the machine-code instructions of a processor. For example, the 6150 processor has a repertoire of 118 instructions compared with double that for the 16-bit Intel 80286 processor.

The 6150 contains a number of novel features including:

- A resource manager to provide a virtual machine interface that conceals the complexities of virtual memory management and input/output devices.
- An 80286 co-processor card that allows users to utilise IBM PC programs without interfering with the normal operation of the 6150.
- A 16-bit input/output channel based on the IBM PC/AT making it possible to use most existing PC/AT attachment cards.

The 6150 was originally aimed at the engineering and CAD marketplace, latterly in the commercial arena. It was not a success in its first year, primarily because of its positioning in the marketplace and also because of users' suspicions concerning IBM's seriousness about UNIX. This has been addressed recently by:

- Further machines being added to the range offering greater processing power and memory at a lower cost.
- IBM's announcement of a strategic commitment to UNIX.
- The availability of commercial application software for the 6150.

It will be interesting to witness the ensuing battle for market supremacy between AT&T (the originators of UNIX) and IBM which has adopted UNIX in competition.

Looking ahead with UNIX

The government of the USA has placed a number of very large orders with various manufacturers where UNIX was specified as the requirement for an operating system. Examples include:

- The US Army (1,800 UNIX based minicomputers)
- The National Security Agency (a $1 billion purchase of AT&T UNIX hardware)
- The Department of Agriculture (a $250 million project to automate central and field offices).

These are in addition to UNIX users already at the Department of Labour and the Inland Revenue Service. There are more departments in the pipeline on the UNIX route. Apart from office automation tasks, such as word-processing, these systems' major use is for database applications specific to the government department, such as client servicing, management and investigation as well as budgeting. In essence these are Decision Support Systems. These systems were also required to have the following characteristics:

- **Distributed systems.** The dispersion of department offices throughout the country necessitated the use of a system capable of distributed processing.
- **Rapid applications development.** The sheer volume of data that has to be processed required a system whereby applications using database management systems and 4GLs could be developed quickly.
- **Software portability.** As new generations of hardware appear, it is necessary that any investment in application software development is not wasted by moving to more powerful hardware.

A further example is the Federal Judicial Center, where UNIX-based decision support systems are being developed for each of the federal courts to monitor the status of court cases, the scheduling of judges and, naturally, the tracking of the volumes of documents that are generated during the course of a trial.

Decision support systems come under the umbrella of MIS. UNIX and 4GLs combined can provide solutions that the MIS manager requires, which can be characterised by:

- Large volumes of data
- Relatively low transaction volumes
- Ability to share data among computers at different locations
- Parts of the total decision support system may reside on different computers at different locations
- Changing requirements, which necessitate that systems be developed incrementally, making a rapid application development environment essential.

It is interesting to note that there are already a number of hardware manufacturers working in conjunction with 4GL vendors to produce UNIX-based systems that can handle very large volumes of transactions. These systems will then be suitable for the very crucial area of online transaction processing systems.

Chapter Thirteen

Databases, Database Management Systems and Fourth-Generation Languages

Most fourth-generation languages are intricately linked to a database. Our purpose in this chapter is to provide an appreciation of the development of databases (in particular relational databases), database management systems and the inevitable progression to 4GLs.

In the early days of data processing, programmers wrote applications software, including the inherent data file handling, as single mammoth systems. This meant that when the next application had to be developed the programmer would develop the system from scratch, including the file handling. The problem was aggravated if the application required access to data files from the previous application, since this usually led to re-structuring the first data file to accommodate the new program. Naturally this state of affairs led to massive data duplication and a jungle of inconsistencies.

There was a requirement for a data management facility where data could be separated from the program, thus allowing programs access to the same set of data files. The solution came in the form of database management systems (DBMS). In essence a DBMS allows data to be looked upon as a physical entity rather than a conceptual one, and also provides access to, and security of, the data.

ANSI/X3/SPARC framework for DBMS

The early database management systems were large and complex because the philosophy associated with them was still being developed. Surprisingly, many still are. The suppliers of such systems had defined their own database model and terminology. In an attempt to examine and provide a basic framework for all future database management systems, a working group was set up in 1971 by the American National Standards Institute (ANSI) and the Committee on Computer and Information Processing (X3) together with the Standards Planning and Requirements Committee (SPARC). The final report appeared in 1978, and has had a far wider implication throughout the information processing industry, primarily because the report proposed the architecture to be independent of any particular data model. (The common data models are the *hierarchical*, *network* and *relational* models which we cover later in the chapter.)

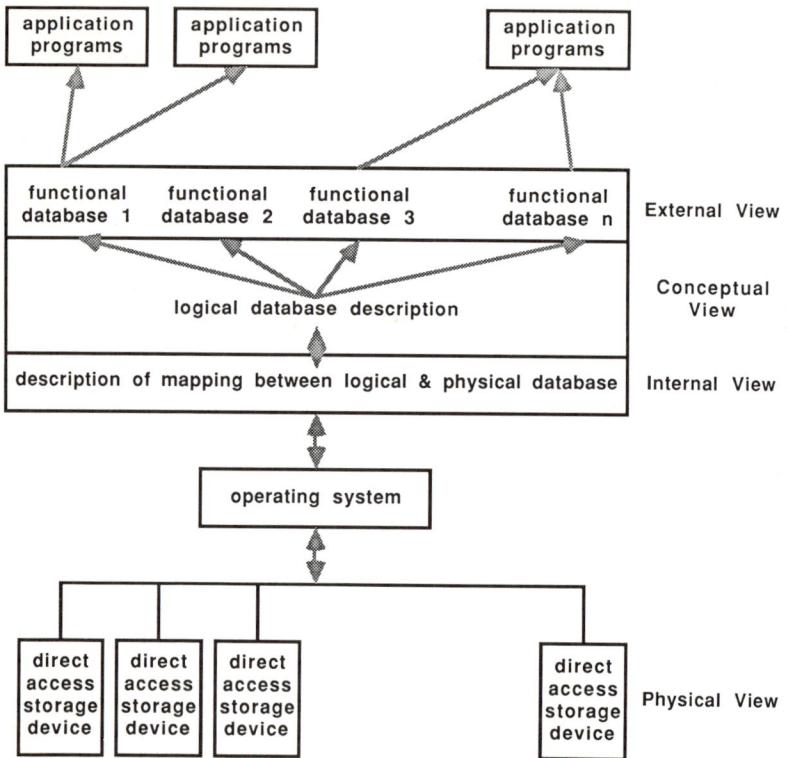

Fig. 13.1   ANSI/X3/SPARC DBMS model.

The framework proposed an architecture comprising three levels (*schemas*) of data abstraction; *external*, *conceptual*, and *internal*. An additional level has been added since, the *physical* level.

External schema
The *external schema* is the level closest to the user. It is the view of the database as seen by the user sitting at a terminal or by an application program. The external schema is also known by the term *functional database*. Under normal circumstances, several applications can use the same functional database, and

there can be many functional databases, each one being described by an external schema definition language.

A number of these languages exist based upon different language constructs. Many of these languages go further than just defining the functional database, they also provide a user interface with the database management software.

Two types of database user

There are basically two type of database user; the *parametric* and the *operational* user. A *parametric user* is one whose transactions on the database are well-defined, and whose only inputs to the system are simple parameters. Airline reservation personnel are an example of parametric users.

An *operational user* is one whose operational requirements are not entirely known. For this reason the functional databases must be constructed at run time by the user using an external schema definition language. A detailed knowledge of the external schema language is required if functional databases are to be created.

Conceptual schema

The *conceptual schema* provides a complete description of the data content of the database. The schema itself is defined by a conceptual schema language, the syntax of which is dependent on the data model chosen.

The conceptual schema defines all the data entities within the database, their attributes, and the logical relationships between them. The conceptual schema is usually the first stage in designing a database system, since it forms the basis for the other levels. Once defined, the conceptual schema should be stable and any changes should reflect only those that occur in the real world; the schema can be modified by extending it to reflect a larger portion of reality. The conceptual schema is also termed the *logical database*, and there can be only one logical database.

Internal schema

The relationship between the logical database and physical storage is defined at the internal level, specifically by the relationship between logical records and storage files. The *internal schema* is a representation of the database at a low level of abstraction. It defines the number of files which constitute the database, their names, logical record length and format, and available access paths.

Physical schema

The physical level is at the very lowest level of abstraction, the level at which data is stored on a storage device. The *physical schema* describes, in terms which are particular to the hardware and software used for creating the database system, the available storage devices, operating system, access methods, characteristics of the physical file and data set. Information would include e.g. the physical record length, key length and offset, block size, file size, and access method.

Putting it together

When an application requests a record, for example, the request is expressed in terms of the functional database. However, the functional database can vary from the actual logical structure of the database. The request is translated from the declarations of the functional database to the declarative structure of the logical database. Once the logical database has received the translated data request, it will then translate it again so that the internal level can determine the actual logical storage of the data to be accessed. This is then finally translated to the access method necessary for the physical database to operate.

Change at one level has minimum effect on other levels

Once these four levels of abstraction are adopted for database design then a modification at any one level will have a minimum effect on all the other levels. Consider, for example, a change to the physical database by the replacement of the disk storage device with one allowing greater capacity and faster access time. Such a change should have no effect on the other three levels, since neither the real world nor the user's requirements have changed. In effect we have:

- Logical data independence; changes in the logical database have a minimal effect on application programs.
- Physical data independence; changes in the physical storage have a minimal effect on the logical database.

Types of database

To gain the maximum benefit from information processing it is essential to have a model from which the data may be viewed. This necessarily implies giving the data a structure. The structure must be flexible enough to allow for various types of data to be defined. A database model is defined as 'an abstract view in which real-world data is logically structured and manipulated within a database'. To date numerous data models have been proposed, but the three predominant ones are the *hierarchical*, *network* and *relational* models.

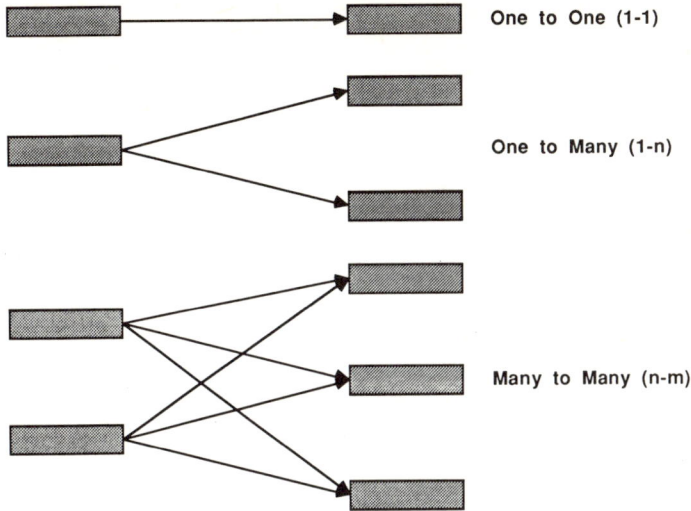

Fig. 13.2 Data relation types.

Hierarchical model

A *hierarchical* structure represents data as tree structures, composed of a hierarchy of records. For example, the UNIX file system is based on the hierarchical model, where every node in the file system has a unique parent and may have a number of children.

The hierarchical model is based on the concept of an 'ownership tree', with each node being either 'owner of' or 'owned by' another. The tree pointers only permit relationships to be retrieved on a one-to-one basis. A one-to-many relationship can only be achieved by the duplication of data. Hierarchical databases have a built-in data integrity check in that no 'child node' may exist without the corresponding 'parent node'. Also, if a given parent node is deleted, then all child nodes associated with that parent will be deleted, automatically. This type of model lends itself to data that is naturally hierarchical. In a hierarchical database the relationship between files and records is explicitly defined and established at the database design stage.

To date the hierarchical database has been the most popular model to implement. One of the reasons for its popularity has been the ease of physical transition from manual to computer system – for example, a filing cabinet is a hierarchy; a cabinet contains drawers, drawers contain files, files contain pages, pages contain data. During the early data processing days, a hierarchy could be implemented conveniently and easily on linear media such as punch cards and magnetic tapes.

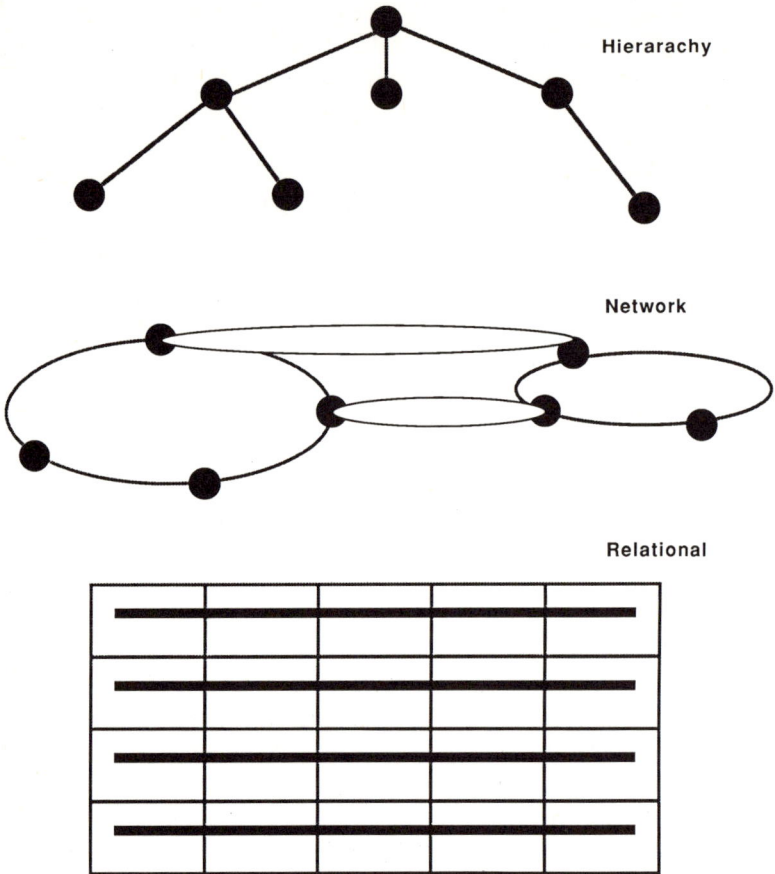

Fig. 13.3 Hierarchical, network and relational models.

The hierarchy model does have some major limitations:

- To find information when the exact location of the record is unknown requires a sequential search of the entire database.
- Information can only exist in one place in a hierarchical database.
- Data has to be duplicated if it is to appear logically in more than one place.
- Changing the structure of a file is not easily accomplished.
- Programs which access the database need to have a complete knowledge of how the data is organised if the tree is to be traversed efficiently.
- Changes in the database structure imply that the access routines within the programs have to be modified.

Network model

The *network* model represents data as records linked together, forming intersecting sets of records. It is loosely based on the concept of 'sets' and solves some of the problems inherent in the hierarchical model by allowing arbitrary pointers. This gives the desirable property of enabling data to appear under more than one heading. For example, the description of the parts making up an assembly could appear in three files; the assembly file, once in each of the files for the parts, and once in each of the files of the manufacturers supplying the parts.

The network structure allows for not only one-to-one and one-to-many relationships but also many-to-many. Many-to-many relationships are set up without the need for data duplication by utilising linked files. This gives each 'child' the ability to have a number of 'parents'. Each occurrence of a given link consists of a single instance of the parent record type and an ordered set of multiple instances of the child type. The pointers linking the files are bi-directional and provide the means of traversing the structure.

One problem with the network model is in the area of deletion. If pointers are used and an item of data is to be deleted, then all the pointers to that data must be found. In practice, network database systems include reference counts and back-pointers so that the deletion of an item of data can also delete all references to that data. The cost of providing such a facility is considerable, both in terms of the programming and processing power needed.

Hierarchy and network models share a common property

The physical representation of data for both hierarchical and network databases is closely associated with the logical organisation of the data. For small applications this is not of much concern, but if the organisation of the data changes in large database systems, all programs that access the data may need to be rewritten.

Relational model

The majority of database management systems currently in the market place (and, by extension, those DBMSs linked to fourth-generation languages) are based on the *relational* database model. It is of value to have an understanding of the relational concept, since it is very much oriented to the way a user perceives data to be structured.

The relational database model was first proposed by Ted Codd in 1979 while he was a scientist at IBM. In the relational model, data is not only independent from programs but also from other data. The relational model has at its core the idea of representing data in *tables* rather than files. Column headings are described as *domains* and items of information as *tuples* or *rows* rather than records.

Relational theory was originally defined in terms of a mathematical model

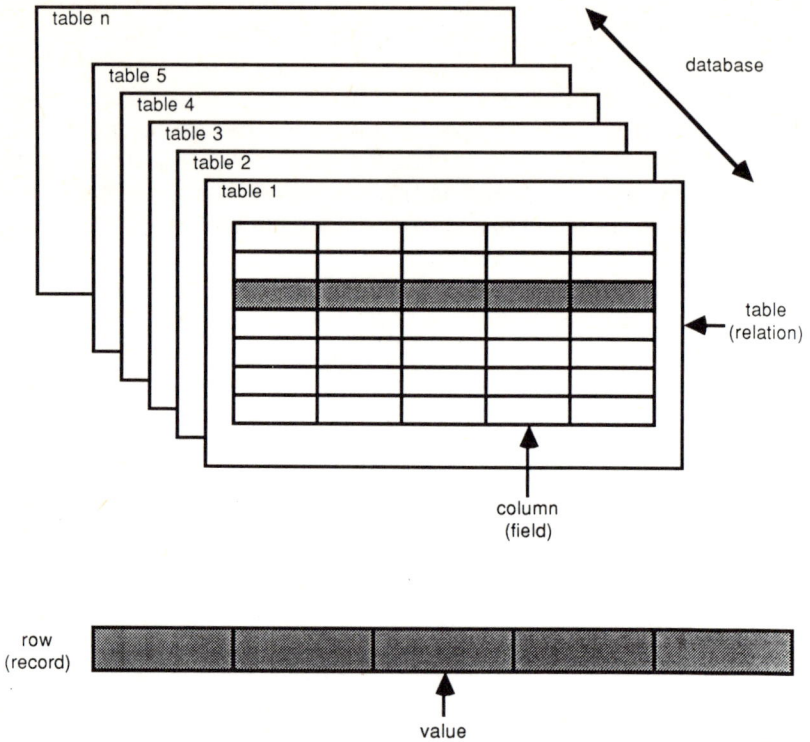

Fig. 13.4 Relational database structure.

for describing the structure of data, and considered much too inefficient to implement practically. It is this background that has surrounded the model with many mathematical concepts and terms.

A relational model removes the constraints regarding the logical relationship between data by reducing all the data to a set of tables or two-dimensional arrays. The model frees the user from artificial constraints, reduces the data relationships to simpler components and represents the components directly in the form of tables. This is the way the user views and stores data on sheets of paper. The ability to define relations and manipulate them via simple but very powerful relational languages is an additional advantage that this model has over the others.

In a relational database, all data is structured as a set of separate tables. These tables are physically unrelated to each other, but they may be logically connected (i.e. by setting up connections between data in one table and data in another table). Considering again the assembly example, one table might contain the list of parts that make up each assembly; another table might contain the list of suppliers that supply each part, etc. Connections are made using logical links; to find the list of suppliers that make parts for a given assembly, first find the set of parts required by the assembly, and then find the list of suppliers that make those parts.

Terminology

A *relation* is a collection of semantically related information. It usually has a unique key associated with it. A relation is referred to as a *table*, since the physical (printed) representation looks like a table of data.

A *tuple* is a single entry in a relation. A tuple is analogous to a record from the data processing environment or a 'row' from the table analogy.

Each individual item of data in a tuple is called an *attribute* or *column*, in conventional terms this is called a *field*.

A *domain* defines a type of data item, and the contents of a column must belong to the same domain for all the rows of the column.

To summarise, and to keep consistency with current terminolgy:

- **Column**; also known as attribute, data item, data element, field.
- **Row**; also known as a tuple, record, entity.
- **Table**; also known as a relation, file, data set, entity set.
- **Database**; a collection of tables.

The main properties of a table representation include:

- All row entries are atomic, i.e. non-divisible
- All entries in a particular column are drawn from the same set.
- Each column has a unique name within the table.
- All rows are distinct.
- Row or column order is not of significance.

The rest of this chapter concerns itself with the relational model, and as such we will use the above relational terminology. We begin with the process of data normalisation.

Normalisation

Normalisation, as first defined by Ted Codd, is a set of rules to be followed sequentially for designing a relational database. Normalisation is a design specification process that seeks to minimise data redundancy and update (insertion, modification, deletion) anomalies in an integrated database. In essence, normalisation addresses the following question:

'What method should be adopted in deciding on the most appropriate logical structure of the data, i.e. what relations are needed and what should their attributes be?'

The object of normalisation is to design specifications that facilitate the enforcement of rules about how attributes are associated. That is, a relation is said to be in a particular 'normal form' if (and only if) it satisfies a particular set of constraints. Normalisation has the following benefits:

• it reduces table maintenance because simpler data structures are enforced
• it improves data integrity
• it reduces data redundancy.

Before we describe the first four normal forms, we a give a brief description of the concept of *keys* in the relational context.

Keys

The notion of keys is of fundamental importance in commercial data processing. We look at a number of *key types* that are part and parcel of the relational model.

A *candidate key* is an attribute or combination of attributes that uniquely identifies a row in a table. There may be more than one candidate key to form the set of candidate keys. The chosen one is the *primary key*. For example in a CUSTOMER relation:

CUSTOMER (salutation, firstname, surname, address, postcode, telephone number, business type),

the attributes 'customer surname', 'telephone number', and 'postcode' would be candidate keys. The combination of 'customer surname' and 'telephone number' is unique, and is therefore a prime candidate for a primary key. In fact, the primary key is a special 'candidate key'. Once a primary key is chosen from the set of candidate keys the remaining keys are termed 'alternate keys'.

A relational database consists of separate tables, with logical connections between data in one table and data in another. The connections are recognised by the existence of *foreign keys*. A foreign key of one table is used to cross-reference with the primary key of another table. The foreign key is that attribute that appears in both tables, and thus allows cross-referencing between two primary keys from distinct but related tables. For example, consider a STUDENT and COURSES relation:

STUDENT (student-number, student-name, student-age, course-number)

COURSES (course-number, course-name, course-department, course-lecturer)

In the STUDENT relation the unique 'student-number' is clearly the primary key, and the 'course-number' is the primary key in the COURSES relation. Also, the 'course-number' is found in both relations, and as such would be the foreign key for the STUDENT relation allowing cross-referencing to the COURSES relation.

The selection of keys is simplified when the normalisation process is applied.

First normal form

A relation is said to be in *first normal form* if all the attributes are atomic, i.e. each attribute is simple and non-divisible. For example, in an EMPLOYEE database, consider a table holding information on each employee's previous position:

PREVIOUS-POSITION (name, position, dates).

This relation is not in first normal form, since 'dates' can be sub-divided into 'start' and 'finish'.

Second normal form

The *second normal form* requires a definition of 'functional dependence' among attributes; an attribute A is functionally dependent on attribute B if for any given value of B there is an associated unique value of A.

A relation is said to be in second normal form if every non-key attribute is functionally dependent on the whole of the primary key. In the COURSES relation, 'course-department' is functionally dependent on 'course-lecturer'. As a further example consider an Airline Ticket Reservation database, and in particular the FLIGHT-AVAILABLE relation:

FLIGHT-AVAILABLE (date, destination, price, seats, seats-available)

This relation is in first normal form but not in second normal form (unless the fare varies from day to day), because the 'price' depends only on the 'destination'. The normalised relations would be:

SEATS (date, destination, seats, seats-available)
FARES (destination, price)

Transitive dependence

An attribute A is *transitively dependent* upon attribute C if A is functionally dependent on attribute B and B is functionally dependent upon C.

Third normal form

A relation is said to be in *third normal form* if it is in second normal form and excludes all transitive dependencies among non-key attributes. In other words, a relation is said to be in third normal form if all non-key attributes are both mutually independent (an attribute can be changed without affecting any other attribute), and fully dependent on the primary key.

The third normal form was found to be unsatisfactory when dealing with relations that had multiple candidate keys that were composite and overlapped. The definition was improved by R. F. Boyce and ended up by being called the Boyce-Codd Normal Form (BCNF). This says that a relation is in BCNF if every *determinant* (an attribute that determines the value of another attribute) is a candidate key.

Relational operations

The relational model has brought with it a number of other operations with associated terminology, in particular relational algebra and relational calculus. Relational algebra is a procedural language in which the user specifies the operation to be performed – but this contains no reference to the access paths, so the specification is independent of how relations are stored.

Relational calculus is a non-procedural query language in which the user specifies the properties of the information to be operated on rather than the detailed steps by which the operation is to be achieved. It is the DBMS that analyses and performs the necessary operations to satisfy the request.

Relational algebra

Relational algebra is a 'functional' language in that each operation returns as its result a relation. The manipulation of relations is conducted through the use of relational algebraic operators, such as 'select', 'projection' and 'join'. We consider each of these:

- **Select** is the simplest and can be thought of as choosing one or more rows from a relation.
- **Projection** produces a specific attribute from a given relation
- **Join** builds another relation (C) from two given relations (A and B) such that the resulting relation contains concatenated pairs of records (from A and B) that satisfy a given condition.

Relational Calculus

Relational algebra and the relational calculus are equivalent; the difference is that the relational calculus exhibits a natural query interface. It is the relational calculus that has led to the large variety of Query Languages that are supported by most commercial DBMSs. The query language determines the ease with which a database can be interrogated.

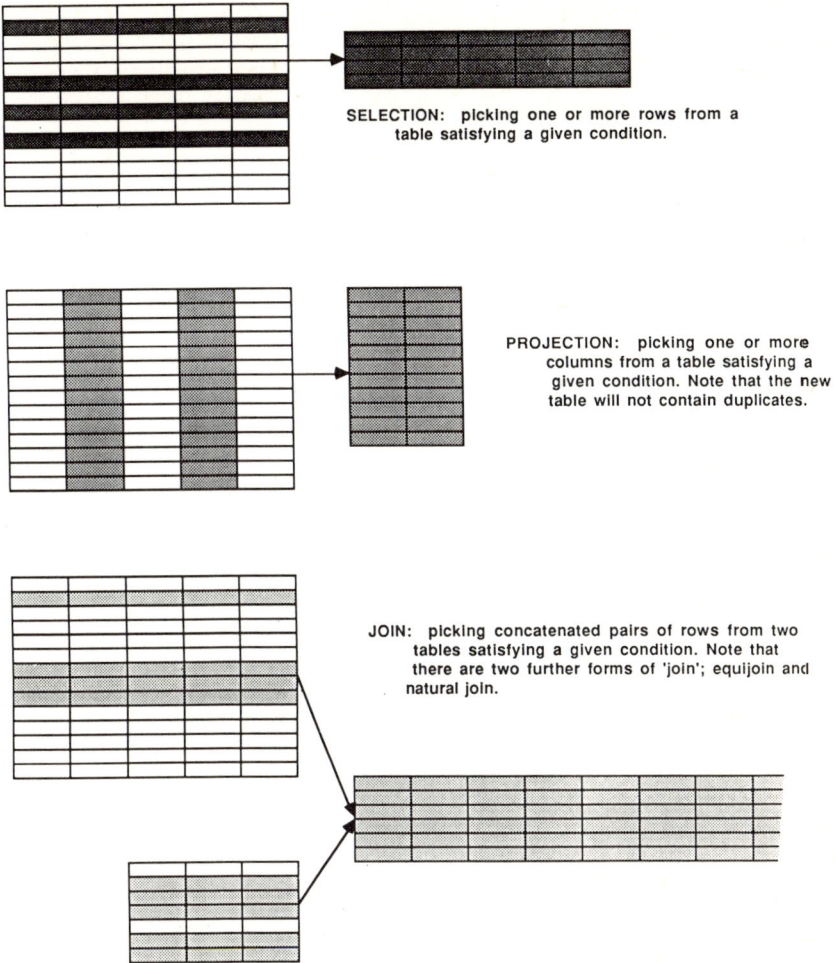

SELECTION: picking one or more rows from a table satisfying a given condition.

PROJECTION: picking one or more columns from a table satisfying a given condition. Note that the new table will not contain duplicates.

JOIN: picking concatenated pairs of rows from two tables satisfying a given condition. Note that there are two further forms of 'join'; equijoin and natural join.

Fig. 13.5 Conceptual views of selection, projection and join.

Key features of a relational DBMS

There are a number of key points about relational databases:

- The language used to access data is non-procedural (that is, it describes what data is wanted rather than how to get the data).

- The language is set-oriented rather than data-oriented.
- Efficient search algorithms are essential to support the relational model.
- Key data is duplicated.
- The database structure can be changed in a way that is transparent to the user.

Database Management Systems

A database management system is simply a combination of hardware and software allowing a user to employ a number of programs to access a database in an orderly fashion. In order to do this a DBMS must be able to configure a computer system with secondary storage so that it can allow for the definition, creation, storage, updating, archiving and management of a set of integrated files. DBMS exist both for single-user personal computers and for multi-user, multi-tasking computers. The advantages of a DBMS include:

- Data independence between the program (logical view of data) and the data (physical database).
- Minimising data redundancy, i.e. the unnecessary duplication of data.
- Data security to protect data from unauthorised access.
- Concurrency control to handle simultaneous users in a multi-user environment.
- Transaction control to preserve data integrity if a transaction fails.
- Provision for easier access to the data for ad hoc questions via report generators and query languages, which in turn reduces the number of applications that have to be coded by programmers.
- DBMS store more information in the same amount of space in a database than in a file system by the use of database pointers.
- The management of data is more efficient with a DBMS because of minimised data redundancy, and maintenance of the database is performed separately from application programs.

The major drawbacks to a DBMS include:

- Centralised information. The failure of the DBMS, either through hardware or software, can cause major losses.
- If a failure occurs then the recovery process is more complex if a large number of users had been accessing the database prior to the failure.

Data dictionary

The concept of a data dictionary is central to the majority of relational database management systems currently available. It is very much the conceptual schema as defined in the ANSI/X3/SPARC framework. Such a data dictionary is also termed an *asset dictionary* because it seeks to build reusable information assets – assets which can be used quickly and easily to build applications in response to changing user requirements.

The data dictionary can contain screen formats, report formats, dialogue structures, associations between many types of data, validity checks, security controls, access permissions, derived field calculations, permissible ranges, and logical relationships among data values. The asset dictionary is a tool to integrate the planning, design, construction and support of an information system. Data dictionaries have evolved to a point where they can be used in many stages of the systems development life-cycle, in order to support application development and maintenance. They can also be employed by users who wish to access data stored in distributed, heterogeneous systems. Data resource management is of fundamental importance within an organisation, and the data dictionary is the tool to aid the task. A data dictionary is the ultimate repository for data in an organisation.

DBMS functions

The primary task of a DBMS is to ensure that efficient and flexible data processsing facilities are provided without compromising data validity. Such facilities include flexible data access paths and a powerful data manipulation language. Secondly, a DBMS should support administration functions that ease database design, optimise utilisation, and minimise maintenance.

Access methods

Access methods allow users and applications flexible paths to the stored data. Access methods are very much dependent on the type of storage structure chosen for the data. The choice of storage structure is critical since it has an effect on the overall performance of the database. It also affects disk space requirements and concurrency. The storage structures supported by the majority of DBMS are *hash*, *ISAM* and *B-tree*.

- **Hashing** can be described in simple terms as a process whereby a record is stored by transforming the key into an address and storing the record at that address. A record is retrieved by computing the address from the key and then fetching the record at that address. Hashing is best used when the data to be retrieved is based on the exact value of the key and data sets are small. The result in such cases is usually faster than either ISAM or B-trees.
- **ISAM (Indexed Sequential Access Method)** is a static indexing method that

maintains a sorted index, very much like that of a book. ISAM is best used when:

- The table is growing slowly
- The key is large
- Queries involve pattern matching and range searches
- The table is small enough to modify frequently.

- **B-trees** are dynamic indices; as records are added the index structure grows. It also provides access to the data sorted by key. B-trees are far more complex to implement than other indexing methods but give a greater overall performance. B-trees are best utilised when:

  - The table is growing rapidly
  - The table is too large to modify regularly
  - Queries require pattern matching and range searches.

Data Manipulation Language

A *Data Manipulation Language* (DML) provides for a non-procedural interface for users to query the data. Non-procedural implies that programs cannot be written with the language. Rather, query languages allow users to ask questions about data values stored in the database, and the DBMS determines the operations needed to satisfy the requests. Query languages are aimed to be used both by users and by application software developers. Users can use the query language to ask questions easily and rapidly. Application developers can use the language during the development stage to verify the results of application programs and to check the validity of stored data. We concentrate here on *SQL* (Structured Query Language), which was developed by IBM. Currently SQL is an ANSI standard and as such is rapidly becoming the industry standard. Even those DBMS that have had a proprietary query language are either replacing it with SQL or providing SQL as an option.

SQL

SQL is a language that both user and developer can employ to query a database as well as operate on the contents of tables. Database management system developers usually supply versions of SQL that do not follow the standard, and as such there is considerable variation among different implementations of SQL. We can only hope that they will soon adhere to the ANSI standard.

SQL is used for a variety of functions including:

- Creating tables

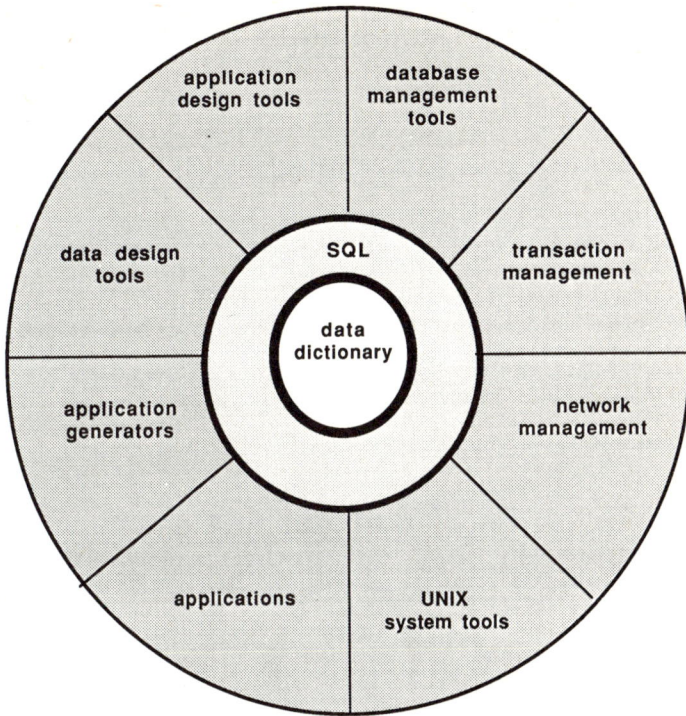

Fig. 13.6 An SQL based DBMS.

- Selecting data from single and multiple tables
- Modifying, inserting and deleting data.
- Performing global changes
- Performing computations using string, set, numeric, date, type conversion and system functions.

The SQL language is very rich in its functionality and available commands, for instance:

- **ALTER TABLE** allows changes to the data dictionary
- **COMMIT WORK** confirms a transaction as complete
- **CREATE INDEX** allows an index to be added to an existing table
- **CREATE TABLE** allows the creation of a new table
- **DELETE** allows for the deletion of a record from a table
- **INSERT** allows for the insertion of a record into a table
- **ROLLBACK WORK** undoes a partially completed transaction
- **SELECT** allows for queries on the database

- **UPDATE** allows an existing record to be changed

Each command has an associated syntax, for example:

- The syntax for CREATE is:

  CREATE TABLE [locationname:] tablename
  (columnname format <,columnname format>);

- The SELECT statement is the most complex, but a simplified version of the syntax is;

  SELECT [ALL : DISTINCT] [result-column =] expression
  <,[result-column =] expression>
  FROM table
  [WHERE search-condition];

  E.g. to find every employee whose name begins with 'Joe', the statement would be formed as:
  SELECT name FROM emp WHERE name = 'Joe*'

Data validity

Data validity is of crucial importance when considering a DBMS. The issues of concern are:

- Data integrity
- Data security
- Concurrency control.

Data integrity
Data integrity is concerned with ensuring that data values are correct. Preserving data integrity can be viewed from two stances. Firstly it must be ensured that data is not corrupted by hardware or software failures. Secondly, it must be ensured that data entered into a database does not violate user-supplied data specifications. A DBMS usually includes a method by which integrity rules can be specified. A rule consists of three parts:

(1) The conditions under which the integrity should be applied.
(2) The condition that is to be tested.
(3) The action to take if (2) is found to be false.

Once data integrity has been defined for the data then the enforcement of the integrity rules is handled by the DBMS, assuring consistency.

Data security
It is desirable that access to data is restricted to authorised users and applications.

The level of security required for any particular database application varies. Users usually require access to different parts of the database, yet allowing users access to all data makes data security more difficult. Most DBMS limit access to data on the user's needs and thus reduce unauthorised access. A secure DBMS will normally provide for access permissions at the:

- database level
- table level and
- row level.

Concurrency control

A multi-user DBMS must meet the following, often conflicting, objectives:

- **Concurrency**. Allow as many users as possible to access and update data whenever they want.
- **Concurrency control**. At the same time each user must be given the impression that they are the only ones updating the database.

If two or more processes are operating at the same time on a particular part of the database, it is important that they do not interfere with each other. Concurrency control is not only vital but must be properly synchronised. If the processes are only retrieving data, unwanted interactions will not occur. The difficulties arise when data updating is performed. What is required is the orderly management of multiple users using the same parts of the database simultaneously. The usual solution to this problem is data locking. DBMS usually provide a *lock manager* to control access to objects in the database during a transaction so that concurrent transactions do not interfere with each other. There are two main types of lock:

- An **S-lock** (shared lock) allows any number of transactions to read a data object and prevent all other transactions from writing to it during the duration of the transaction. Others can read the data object, but not write to it. An S-lock is also referred to as a *read lock* or *advisory lock*.
- An **X-lock** (exclusive lock) on data objects associated with a single transaction prevents others from reading or updating the same data objects. An X-lock is also referred to as a *write lock* or *mandatory lock*.

A lock manager will usually provide locks to be set at three levels. The application will decide which level to use and this is dependent on the integrity requirements. The levels are:

- **Database level lock**: this will allow a single process access to the database, disabling use to all others (e.g. during a backup procedure or database restoring).
- **Table level lock**: this will allow locks to be set on the whole of a table (e.g.

in a report or batch update program, where it might be necessary to examine or update entire tables).

- **Row level lock**: this will allow locks to be set on a row in a table. It is the most complex of the levels to implement but a minimum requirement for commercial applications. An additional feature usually provided is the ability to lock a set of rows exclusively.

Waiting for a lock by two users performing transactions on EMP(loyee) and DEPT(artment) tables. Each step is numbered in the order of execution.

	USER 1		USER 2
1.	begin transaction	2.	begin transaction
3.	update record in EMP table	4.	update same record in EMP table
	X-lock on EMP table		must wait for X-lock on EMP table
5.	select record from DEPT table	7.	proceed with transaction
	S-lock on DEPT table		
6.	end transaction	8.	end transaction
	release locks		

Fig. 13.7 Example of waiting for a lock.

Deadlock

Locks are released when the process terminates. This appears simple enough but it can lead to a *deadlock* situation. Consider the following scenario. Processs P1 has locked table A, and needs a lock on table B. At the same time process P2 has locked table B and needs a lock on table A. Deadlock occurs because neither process can proceed. There are two possible solutions to the deadlock problem:

(1) Let a process lock all resources required before allowing it to start. The disadvantage to this method is that a process may not *know* what it is going to need until it has started running.

(2) Monitor the possibility of deadlock and act upon it when it occurs. If two or more processes are stalled for a certain period of time, then assume that deadlock has occured.

One way out of the deadlock situation is to *rollback* one or more transactions. That is, the system 'undoes' any transactions the process has performed and frees resources that had been locked. The process is then placed on a queue to be restarted later.

Rollback

Apart from the above scenario for detecting deadlock and then using

Deadlock situation caused by two users performing transactions on EMP(loyee) and DEPT(artment) tables. Each step is numbered in the order of execution.

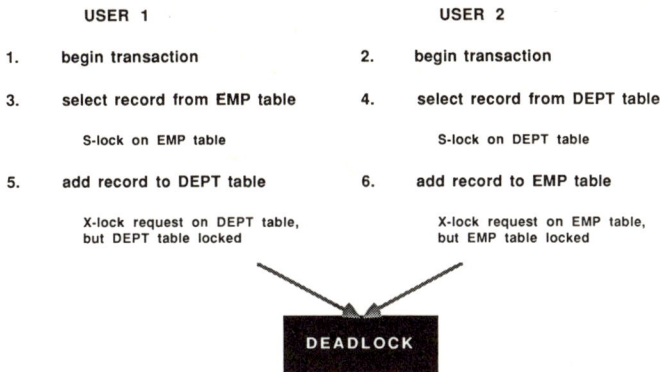

USER 1		USER 2
1.	begin transaction	2.	begin transaction
3.	select record from EMP table	4.	select record from DEPT table
	S-lock on EMP table		S-lock on DEPT table
5.	add record to DEPT table	6.	add record to EMP table
	X-lock request on DEPT table, but DEPT table locked		X-lock request on EMP table, but EMP table locked

DEADLOCK

Both users will be unable to continue until one transaction is aborted, allowing the other to proceed.

Fig. 13.8   Example of a deadlock situation.

rollback, there are two further situations where rollback is employed in DBMS to ensure that complete transactions are applied to the database:

(1) Most DBMSs will apply transaction updates as they occur, so that if the operator aborts the transaction halfway through, the DBMS can then physically reverse the updates by the use of rollback.
(2) If the hardware goes down during the course of updating, the data could be left in an inconsistent state. Applying rollback will return to the last completed transaction. We cover this later under backup and recovery.

Some DBMS also support *roll forward*, where files are restored to the last backup and are then rolled forward a transaction at a time from there on.

Lock manager requirements
The minimum requirements of a lock manager within a multi-tasking, multi-user operating system environment should include:

• Support of both shared and exclusive locks
• Locking at the database, table and row level
• Locking implemented in shared memory. The lock status of an object must be accessible to all transactions, since this is a requirement for concurrent control.
• No upper limit to the number of locks per transaction. Databases with hundreds of thousands of records and dozens of users may need to lock

very large numbers of data objects (the *limit problem*).

• Support of lock promotion. Since memory is usually at a premium, the locking mechanism must have some method of memory conservation to allow transactions that require large numbers of locks to run successfully.

UNIX locking revisited

UNIX System V Release 3.0 provides for both shared and exclusive locks. The basic unit of UNIX locking is the byte, so that database, table, and record level locks can be set as well as 'set of records' locks. Shared memory is available to UNIX users in three ways:

• Operating system memory which is shared among all users
• Utilising the inter-process communications facility
• Using the standard UNIX System V shared memory feature.

UNIX, however, does not provide a solution for the *limit problem*. The maximum number of locks is a 'system-wide' limit. It is not a 'per database' or 'per transaction' number. The UNIX system-wide limit is usually between 50 and 100, a very small number for commercial applications. A typical small application in a single-user transaction could lock 100 records, while a medium-sized application could easily need 2,000 simultaneous locks.

UNIX also provides a restricted form of memory conservation. When a lock is requested on bytes adjacent to a lock already held by the same transaction, the locks are merged into a single lock. This is restrictive, since a typical transaction will have records that need locking randomly distributed. What is required is a *lock promotion mechanism*. For example, if N is the current maximum lock limit, and a transaction already has N locks, then the next request for a lock will cause the promotion of a set of lower level locks to the next highest level. For example, a set of record level locks should be promoted to a table level lock, setting free the record level locks at the same time.

Other DBMS considerations

A DBMS will usually keep track of all transactions on the database in a *transaction log file*. In the event of a DBMS failure, database maintenance tools must be provided for the recovery process, specifically tools for *backup*, or archiving, and *restoration* of the database from the backup (or archive). Periodic backups of the database must be taken in case of failure. After the failure of a database, it is restored from the most recent backup. Once restored, the appropriate part of the transaction log is applied to the recovered database, to return it to a state as close as possible to that before failure occurred. An area of concern with this method is the time taken to repeat the entire transaction log.

An alternative solution is to use rollback, which begins with the database in its failed state and attempts to undo all transactions that did not completely finish before failure. Once the database is recovered, the aborted transactions can be modified and resumed. This method is faster, since it works backwards from the point of failure.

The task of database recovery is one of the concerns of the *Database Administrator* (DBA). The DBA (usually a group of people rather than one person) is also responsible, among other things, for:

- database creation
- creation of shareable tables
- database loading
- setting user access permissions
- maintaining the database for performance and tuning when necessary.

Islands of information

In the 1970s, minicomputers were most commonly used for solving departmental needs. In the 1980s PCs increasingly encroached on this territory and brought computing down to the individual user. Since the mid-80s fourth-generation languages have begun to reduce the application backlog.

However, these developments have brought with them some new problems. The most pressing is the dispersion of information over different computing environments, both hardware and software. This state of affairs causes an 'islands of information' syndrome. The answer is networking of both hardware and software, but this involves three basic problems:

- the networked environment needs programming
- the network would not be transparent to the users
- the user would need to know the location of the data required.

The solution lies in products that would give a single, consistent, relational view over an entire system of PCs to minis to mainframes, no matter what the operating system or hardware manufacturer. It would also not matter whether the organisation had a few computers or a few thousand. The product would make it easy to build applications and to share data spanning multiple computers just as easily as if all the data were located on one machine. The machines could be connected by cable, satellite or even over standard telephone lines via modems. Using relational database technology, tables could reside on separate computers in different parts of a building, different parts of a country or different parts of the world. The product would have the necessary intelligence and information to search across multiple computers to find the necessary information.

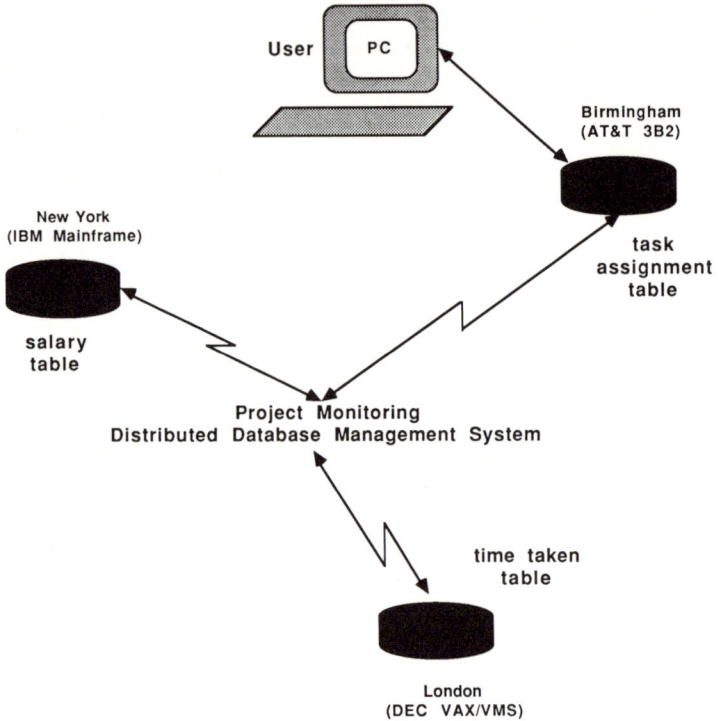

Fig. 13.9 Example of a distributed database management system.

Distributed database management systems

For example, consider a project monitoring system accessed from a PC. The requirement is to find the costs to date associated with a particular project. From the PC one could access the task assignments from one table, the time associated with each task from a second table, and the salary information from a third table. The location of the tables would be transparent to the user on the PC; for example, the 'task assignment' table could be on an AT&T UNIX computer in a regional office in Birmingham, the 'time taken' table on a DEC VAX computer at European headquarters in London, and the 'salary' table on an IBM mainframe at corporate headquarters in New York. Such products would be described as *distributed database management systems*, and what is more they are available now. Global computing has arrived. Distributed DBMS and 4GLs are going to become one of the most important aspects of information strategy for corporations.

Two-phase locking for distributed database systems

Concurrency and locking become an even greater issue in a distributed database environment. The method being chosen by many distributed DBMS developers is an OSI standard (*CCR* – commitment, concurrency, and recovery), and is termed *two-phase locking*. The technique has two distinct phases:

(1) A transaction checks all the records to be updated to ensure that they are available, and then locks them (i.e. locks are acquired).
(2) The process proceeds to the 'commit' stage to confirm the updates (i.e. no new locks are acquired).

Furthermore a transaction is not allowed to release its X-locks until it is ready to commit its actions. At commit, the DBMS guarantees that the updates will take place. In a distributed environment, deadlock detection is more common than deadlock avoidance. Deadlock detection is implemented by using a 'time-out' technique; a transaction is aborted if it exceeds its waiting time.

Towards a fourth-generation language environment

A DBMS and its associated data dictionary is the starting point for the majority of multi-user fourth-generation language environments. As we have seen, a relational DBMS provides the developer and user with a combination of hardware and software that allows the use of a number of programs to access a database in an orderly way. It also provides for a non-procedural language with which to query the database.

The requirement now is to develop application software. As an illustration and reference point, consider a very simplistic program. This would have an input (either from screen or file), processing on the input in association with a file, and output (either onto screen or a report). Using a third-generation language, the developer would have to code the entire application (i.e. screen handling, file handling, computation, logic processing, report generation, etc).

The route to a 4GL environment is provided by tools that are built around the DBMS. The first stage of 4GL development allowed the application developer to produce applications by having 'hooks' to the DBMS via a third-generation language. For example, the majority of UNIX-based DBMS use the C language as the application development language. The developer creates an application by writing programs in C, using function calls into the DBMS. The function calls would allow, for example, the creation, insertion, modification, and deletion of data in the application database.

The second stage involves the provision of a *forms generator* and a *report generator*:

- **Forms generation** allows the developer or user to interactively paint customised screens for use with the application. They would be used, for example, for data insertion, modification and deletion. Default forms for each table in the database are usually available.
- **Report generation** allows for the design of customised reports using either a forms-based procedure or a report-writer definition language to create highly formatted reports. Default reports are usually available.

To do useful work, we need to use the forms created, do some processing, then either display the result using one of the forms created or produce a report via the report writer. Again, in most cases this is achieved by using a third-generation language to integrate the various components; forms, processing and reports.

The third stage provides a non-procedural query language with which both the developer and the user can manipulate the database without recourse to a programming language. The query language enables the user to obtain questions to ad hoc enquiries on the database, as and when needed. Initially each DBMS producer provided a proprietary query language, but these are now being superseded by SQL, the industry standard query language.

The fourth stage on the route to a 4GL environment is a general procedural language that links the forms generator and report generator. These procedural languages are usually proprietary to the 4GL producers, but there is a move among many of them to base it on SQL. Thus one finds that the procedural language used to tie the application together allows for embedded SQL statements. In other words, SQL statements are used to perform operations on the database from within a very general programming language.

The next chapter describes the fourth-generation language environment in greater detail using currently available 4GLs as examples.

Chapter Fourteen
Commercial Fourth-Generation Languages

The DOS operating system has created one of the largest marketplaces for the software developer. The number and variety of applications has been quite staggering in the relatively short time since DOS's introduction. What is more, the software has been unsurpassed in quality. A whole population of workers has been exposed to the robustness, functionality and ease of use exemplified by PC-based products such as Lotus 123 and dBase III. Lotus 123-like user interfaces are the vogue. These same standards are expected in the multi-user arena.

This chapter gives the flavour of the currently available fourth-generation language environments under DOS and UNIX. The products described have been chosen using the following criteria:

- the product is available under both DOS and UNIX, with UNIX being the prime marketing vehicle
- the product has a large market share
- the product exhibits innovative features
- the product has an underlying database management system
- the product is continually being developed to cater for future user and DP requirements, specifically networking and distributed databases.

The aim is to provide an overall functional description (rather than an evaluation) of each product, and a comparison of the advantages and disadvantages of each one. The four products we have chosen are:

(1) Accell
(2) Ingres
(3) Informix/4GL
(4) Oracle.

Accell

Accell is a product from the Unify Corporation in the USA, which is better known for its Unify relational database management system, the leading UNIX-based DBMS in the USA. Accell is a new product, available since early 1986, and is marketed as an 'integrated development system' for building database-oriented transaction processing applications. A version of Unify is available for PCs, but Accell is primarily aimed at the UNIX marketplace, though an Accell PC version is available.

The products can be bought separately depending on the facilities required; however, Accell's underlying relational database management system is in fact the Unify DBMS, and as such the products complement each other. Accell is in essence a forms-driven application development environment using 'windowing' techniques. There are five major integrated components of Accell:

(1) **Accell/DBMS**, a relational database management system.
(2) **Accell/Environment**, which provides an access point to the various parts of Accell.
(3) **Accell/Generator**, a visual application generator used to create forms with windowing features.
(4) **Accell/Language**, a procedural language to add control logic and computation to forms.
(5) **Accell/Manager**, the run-time module that links the forms, language scripts and database tables.

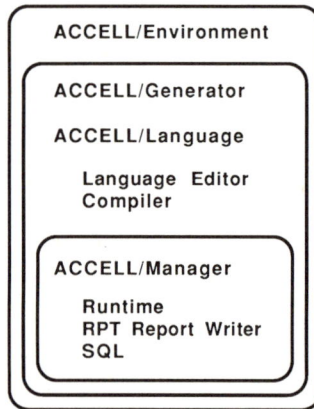

```
┌────────────────────────────────────────┐
│        ACCELL/Environment               │
│  ┌──────────────────────────────────┐   │
│  │   ACCELL/Generator               │   │
│  │                                  │   │
│  │   ACCELL/Language                │   │
│  │                                  │   │
│  │      Language  Editor            │   │
│  │      Compiler                    │   │
│  │  ┌────────────────────────────┐  │   │
│  │  │  ACCELL/Manager            │  │   │
│  │  │                            │  │   │
│  │  │  Runtime                   │  │   │
│  │  │  RPT Report Writer         │  │   │
│  │  │  SQL                       │  │   │
│  │  └────────────────────────────┘  │   │
│  └──────────────────────────────────┘   │
└────────────────────────────────────────┘
```

Fig. 14.1 The Accell environment.

Accell/DBMS

The Accell/DBMS (or Unify DBMS) provides the flexibility of a relational database, an integrated data dictionary, various access methods and transaction logging. It provides a screen-driven facility for defining the structure of a database. A dynamic data dictionary is not available, so changes to table definitions require modifications and recompilation of the whole database system. Accell/DBMS uses fixed length records and the field (attribute) types allowed are numeric, float, string, date, time, amount and a special one termed *comb*, a combination of one or more other fields. The storage structures supported are B-tree indexing, hashing, links and *sequential*. The sequential access method is used when retrieving data from a non-indexed field, or in a search of data involving a scan of all the records in a table. To achieve greater performance, sequential access can be buffered.

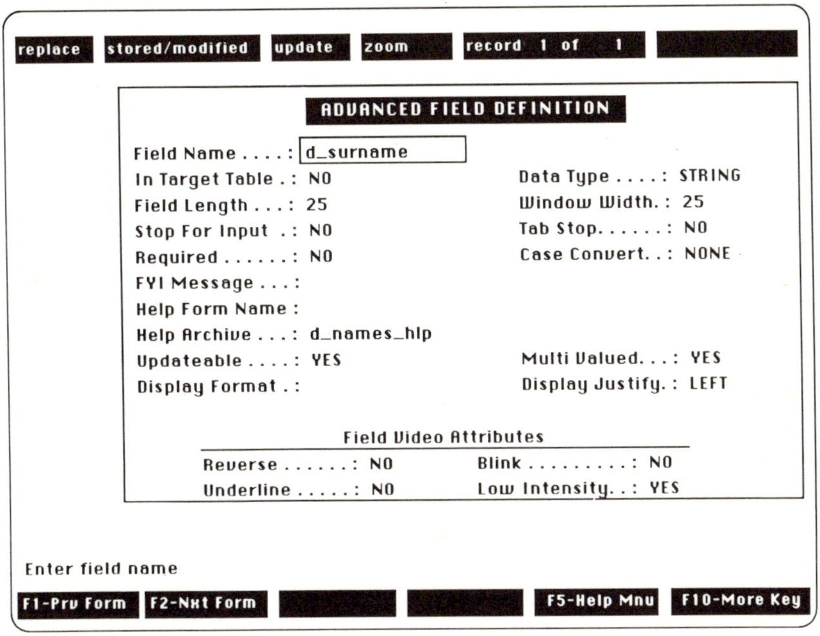

Fig. 14.2   A field definition form in Accell.

Explicit relationships can be set up using *links*. A field in one table can be linked with the primary key of another table, usually termed the *reference table*. Links can be added to the database dynamically, and the benefits associated with linked tables include:

- Speed and efficiency for enquiries on related information in different tables using joins.
- The inability to delete a record in the reference table if there are associated

records in the linked table, providing for 'referential integrity'.
- Validation on input for the linked table will only be accepted if values in the reference table match.

Accell/DBMS uses Unify's *Pathfinder* architecture to determine intelligently which of the access methods will provide the quickest response for a particular query.

The maximum expected table size has to be specified before a table can be created. Initially the DBMS allocates an additional contiguous area one-sixth of the maximum table size given to allow additions greater than those expected. As soon as this reserve area is used up, a further one-sixth of the original area is allocated. This process continues up to a maximum of ten-sixths of the original size. To overcome UNIX's cumbersome file system, Accell can make use of raw disk, providing a far better performance (typically a 40% increase on access speeds).

Accell/Generator

The Accell/Generator is a visual application generation development tool with which an application developer 'paints' screen forms; changes the size, shape and location of windows; defines database fields; defines and locates screen fields; defines screen attributes; and creates default menus. The generator also describes the control-flow between forms. The complete module is interactive and basically follows the current vogue of WYSIWYG (What You See Is What You Get).

The screen format facilities of Accell are its most distinctive feature. A wide range of effects is possible, but the most innovative is 'zoom' – by pressing a special key, a window can be opened on the screen in which the contents of a reference file can be displayed, allowing the user to 'zoom' around different forms. These are only two of a wide range of possibilities.

Using the generator, simple applications can be set up very quickly. For a run-time application a language script is automaticaly generated for each form created. If an application requires complex logic and computations then the language script can be edited to add in the required complexity.

Accell/Language

The Accell/Language allows the developer to:

- Add control logic and computation to a form and provide for user interaction
- Operate on database tables
- Combine information from different tables into one form.

The language module works in conjunction with the generator module in a 'programming by exception' mode. That is, the language should only be used

1. **Select Current Application**

2. **Select Current Form**

3. **Select Action**

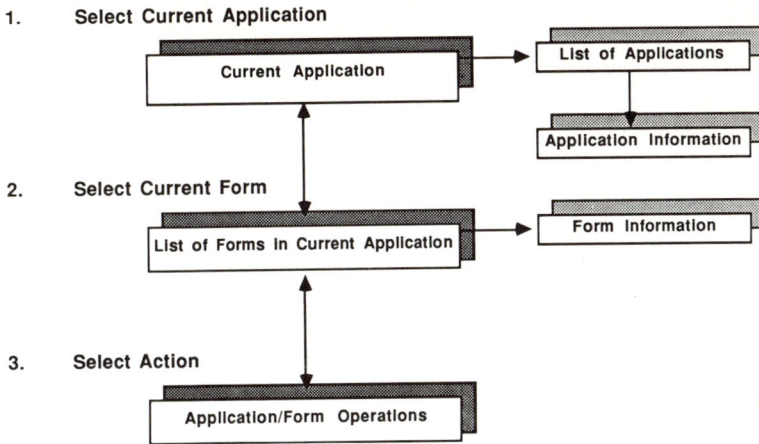

Fig. 14.3 Application creation using the Accell/Environment.

when the developer has to use it. The language is non-procedural in nature, requiring only a few hours' training. An interface is provided to third-generation languages, in particular the 'C' language. The Accell/Language is structured and a large selection of keywords is available. SQL-like statements can be embedded within the language script. The language can be used on its own, like the generator, permitting applications to be developed using this module only.

Application development using the Accell/Language

An application must first be named and defined. Every named application has one source file which is automatically created by the Accell/Environment, and can be modified using a standard editor and then compiled. Screen development takes place within an application. On entering the Accell/Environment, the application being worked has to be specified, allowing the developer to define specific forms. Each form within an application has a corresponding Accell/Language script created automatically by the Accell/Generator, which can be modified using a standard editor. For each form, Accell allows the facility to define any other associated form or forms required.

An Accell/Language program is composed of one or more standard code 'sections'. The code sections specify statements to be executed:

- when the user presses the 'clear to add' key
- when the value of a field changes

- when the cursor moves to a new field
- when the user moves to the next form
- before the first form appears
- after the application ends.

An application source file is composed of two types of section; a MASTER FORM section, and a STANDARD FORM section which can be repeated as many times as required. The MASTER FORM section is very much the application initialiser and the language sections include:

- **BEFORE APPLICATION,** used to establish the user's identity, initialise application totals, establish security constraints, etc.
- **AFTER APPLICATION,** which describes the actions to take before exiting the application, and can include tasks such as displaying messages, displaying summary statistics, updating totals, etc.
- **CHOOSE FIRST FORM,** allows the developer to specify the first standard form or forms to be used.

The STANDARD FORM sections allow for the following self-explanatory keywords, which constitute a language section:
- **BEFORE FORM**
- **CHOOSE NEXT FORM**
- **ON NEXT FORM**
- **ON PREVIOUS FORM**
- **AFTER ZOOM**
- **ON CLEAR TO ADD**
- **BEFORE ADD**
- **AFTER ADD**
- **BEFORE FIND**
- **ON FIND**
- **AFTER FIND**
- **BEFORE UPDATE**
- **AFTER UPDATE**
- **BEFORE DELETE**
- **AFTER DELETE.**

Within each language section, keywords are available for operating on fields, including:

- **INIT**(ialise) **FIELD**
- **BEFORE FIELD**
- **ON FIELD**
- **AFTER FIELD**
- **WHEN FIELD CHANGES.**

The various sections are actioned as required depending on the commands issued by the user. To summarise, Accell/Language files contain one or more code sections, and each code section contains one or more Accell/Language statements. There are three types of statement:

- **Screen statements** let the developer define screen and form attributes, for example blinking, reverse video, underline, case conversion etc.
- **Control statements** allow for logical processing with the use of statements such as:
  - **SET, IF, FOR, WHILE, REPEAT, SWITCH.**
  - **COMMIT TRANSACTION, REJECT RECORD, REJECT OPERA-TION, NEXT ACTION, RESTART ON FIELD.**
  - **ENABLE ZOOM, DISABLE ZOOM.**

  - Database statements allow operations on the database to take place by using statements including:

  - **UPDATE CURRENT RECORD, DELETE CURRENT RECORD.**
  - **INSERT.**
  - **DELETE TABLE.**
  - **XLOCK, SLOCK, UNLOCK.**

Also external function routines written in the 'C' language can be called from the Accell/Language script.

Accell/Environment

It is through the Accell/Environment that an application developer can edit the Accell/Language scripts, view the generator forms and run the application in the prototype mode. A preprocessor within the environment (consisting of a precompiler, combiner and archiver) offers the developer a one-step-at-a-time merging of forms and the language into a completed application.

The sequence to follow when using the Accell/Environment is:

(1) Select the current application from the list of applications.
(2) Select the current form within the chosen application.
(3) Select one of the following options:

- Edit Accell/Generator Form
- Edit Accell/Language Script
- Compile/Integrate Forms, Language Script
- Run Application
- Compile/Integrate/Run Application
- Operating System Commands

Each application has associated with it an 'application information' form giving:

- the directory name
- time of creation
- time of last modification
- number of forms
- description.

Also each form has an associated 'form information' form giving information on the form and the corresponding language script:

- form file name
- time of creation of form
- time of last modification of form
- size of form file in bytes
- language script name
- time of creation of script
- time of last modification of script
- size of script in bytes
- description.

If an application has to be modified during development, the developer will start the preprocessor, and only those forms that have been altered with the new language script are processed. This provides a decrease in this portion of the development cycle. The preprocessor also provides the necessary binding before an application is completed at the run-time stage by the Accell/ Manager.

The prototype mode lets the developer watch the workings of the application while it is running. It allows the developer to view the application as the user views it. It provides access to Accell/Language commands to control the application, allowing the developer to set conditional breakpoints, fixed breakpoints, arbitrary variables, attribute settings etc. All returned values are displayed within a window on the screen.

Accell/Manager

The Accell/Manager handles the run-time interaction between the application and the user. It combines the strengths of table-driven, precompiled and interpreted approaches. In essence the Accell/Manager interprets the user's commands at the keyboard, calls up the various forms in the right order, and executes compiled 4GL statements as required. Applications are run in one of two standard modes: 'find' and 'add/delete/update'. Modes can be changed at any time using function keys or from within a language script.

Accell applications are compiled to a special format (unusually, Accell also compiles embedded SQL-like statements) which is then used by the Accell/

Manager – the run-time environment. The Accell/Manager runs applications under UNIX as a single process, i.e. each user has a single process running. However, processes run the same re-entrant program, so that only one copy of the program code is held in memory.

The Accell/Manager also allows **help** screens to be set up when painting screens. Messages can be created for each attribute on the form. During run-time a help screen for a form is activated when the 'help key' is pressed.

Query by forms and report writer

Forms employed by the user (and the developer) for entering data are used by Accell to provide 'query by forms' (QBF). QBF lets the user define queries by entering fields with the search values, strings or ranges he wishes to use.

RPT is the Accell/DBMS report writer that allows the user to produce tailored reports. Features supported include multiple-line titles and column headings, arithmetic functions, page headers and footers, and conditional 'IF-THEN-ELSE' processing. Default reports are not supported. Unfortunately, at the moment RPT has to be set up manually by creating a script, rather than by using an on-screen 'paint' facility.

Accell development cycle

An application development cycle using Accell can take the following sequence:

- Define the relational database structure via the Accell/DBMS.
- Enter the Accell/Environment and paint forms by using Accell/Generator. Set the size and location of form windows, set the form attributes and establish the control-flow between forms and menus.
- Switch windows to the Accell/Language and create a script to optimise the flow of control between forms. If complex logic and computations are required, then add them at this stage.
- Switch back to the Accell/Environment and initiate the one-step preprocessor to merge the forms and language script into a unified application.
- Begin running the application in the prototype mode to ensure that all functions are working correctly as a whole.
- Let users have access to the prototype and collect feedback. Once feedback is obtained refine the application by modifying data structures, forms, and logic. Reprocess the application and let users have access to the system again. Repeat this process until user satisfaction is obtained. This step should also take into account requests from users for enhancements.
- Prepare final system to run under the Accell/Manager run-time module and install system for users' use.

Ingres

Ingres, an acronym for INtegrated Graphics and REtrieval System, is the outcome of a research project at the University of California at Berkeley in the early 1970s. The first version from Berkeley was made available in 1975. Ingres is currently developed and produced by Relational Technology of California, which was incorporated in 1980 to commercially market Ingres. The initial development was under UNIX, but was later transferred onto DEC's VMS operating system where it has the largest concentration of users. The product line encompasses a full spectrum of operating systems from personal computers (DOS) to minicomputers (UNIX, VMS) and mainframes (VM/CMS).

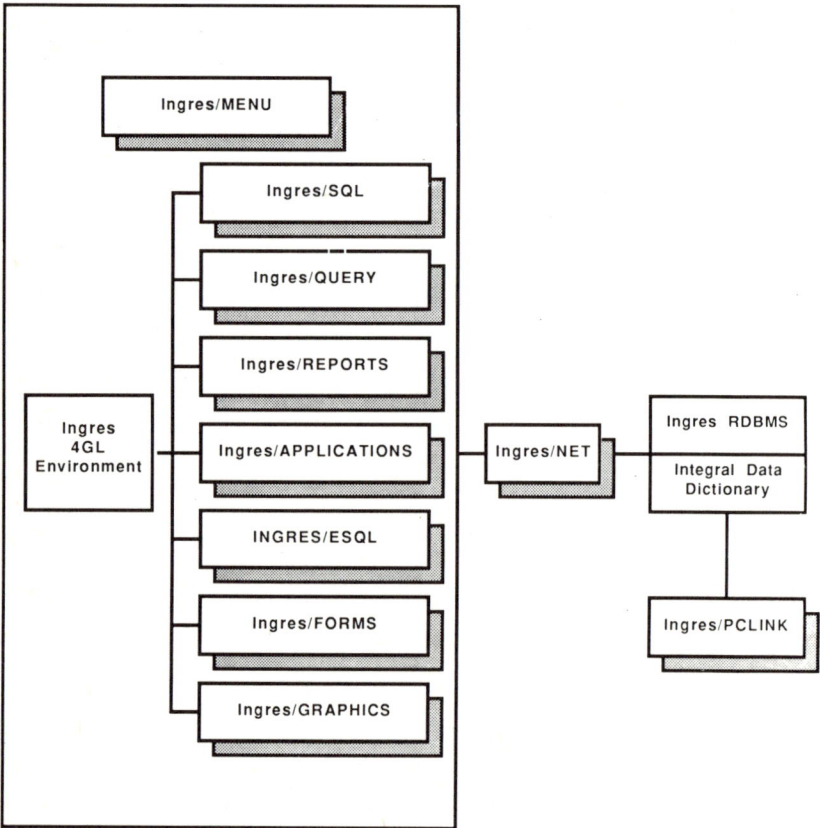

Fig. 14.4 Ingres subsystems.

Ingres is composed of a number of subsystems as follows:

- **Ingres/SQL**, an interactive query language.
- **Ingres/QUERY**, the query by forms module.
- **Ingres/FORMS**, a visual forms editor.
- **Ingres/REPORTS**, the report writer.
- **Ingres/ESQL**, embedded SQL facility.
- **Ingres/GRAPHICS**, basic graphics including pie, bar and scatter.
- **Ingres/APPLICATIONS**, the applications by forms (ABF) module.

In addition, Ingres can be implemented over a network under VMS and UNIX (Ingres/NET) and a distributed database facility is provided by Ingres/STAR. There is also not only a facility to extract and manipulate data via a PC (Ingres/PCLINK) but a stand-alone PC version of Ingres (Ingres/PC).

Ingres structures

Each Ingres table is composed of 'pages', and each page is 2K long. Pages are divided into records with the proviso that records are not allowed to span pages. The record length is equal to the width of a row of a table, and the number of records on a page is dependent on the record width and on the storage structure used.

Ingres uses fixed-length records and supports four types of storage structures. ISAM, B-tree, hashing and *heap*. Heap is the default storage structure, and is used for sequential data entry and access. It is best used when loading large amounts of data into the database and when a table is only one or two pages of data, since it is the only storage structure that does not use keys.

Field types can be integer, character, vchar, floating point, date, time, and money. The special *vchar* type of field allows spaces to be stored in such a way that they appear on output but are ignored when performing searches.

Process structure

Two processes are used on Ingres for each user; a front-end application process that is visible to the user and a back-end data process. The back-end process is actually the database manager which supports all modules, programs, and utilities and coordinates communication between the user and the data. Communication is performed by sending SQL statements in one direction and data in the other.

There are two ways of accessing an Ingres database:

- selecting Ingres subsystems from Ingres/MENU
- calling from within an Ingres application.

Ingres/MENU

Developers and users are faced with the Ingres/MENU module on entering the Ingres system. Ingres/MENU acts as an all-encompassing shell around the rest of the system to provide a consistent user interface. It keeps a single back-end process running all the time while performing any number of front-end processes. It also keeps a history of a user's operations, which facilitates review and repetition.

The commands available from Ingres/MENU are:

- **QUERY**, to run, retrieve, modify or append data via a form.
- **REPORT**, to run a default or saved report.
- **RUNGRAPH**, to run a saved graph defined by VIGRAPH.
- **QBF**, (query by forms) to develop and test query definitions.
- **RBF**, (report by forms) to design or modify reports.
- **VIGRAPH**, to design, modify or test graphs.
- **ABF**, (application by forms) to design and test applications.
- **TABLES**, to create, manipulate or look up tables in the database.
- **VIFRED**, to edit forms using the visual forms editor.
- **SQL**, to enter interactive SQL statements.
- **SREPORT**, to save report writer commands.

VIFRED (VIsual FoRms EDitor)

The visual forms editor allows the user or developer to edit forms. In Ingres a 'frame' defines a screen, which is broken down into a 'form' defined as a two-dimensional object displayed on a terminal screen, and an 'operations menu' at the bottom of the screen. A form in turn comprises a 'trim' (a one-line string of characters used for annotation) and a 'field' which is used for data entry. The trim does not necessarily have to be associated with any field. A field is further broken down into three parts; the 'title' of the field, the 'data window' where data is entered, and the 'attribute' which provides for any special display or data validation feature to be set. The bottom line of the screen shows the commands allocated to the function keys. Help screens can be set for each screen within the application.

Ingres forms can be larger than the physical screen size, in both directions. It is possible to define the order in which various fields are to be traversed when entering data and (especially useful for one-character input) whether or not the return key has to be hit after each field entry.

The use of forms runs throughout the Ingres system. Once a table is created, a default form is automatically created. This form can be used as is, or edited to provide one to the developer's and users' taste. A form, once created, can be used to insert, update, or delete records from the table. The same form can also be used in conjunction with 'query by forms' (QBF) to make enquiries on the database.

Query by forms (QBF)

Ingres allows a query by forms (QBF) facility whereby the user can enter fields using standard screen forms and the records satisfying the criteria will be found. Forms can be created (via VIFRED) for three types of query target:

(1) **Tables**
(2) **JoinDef** (one or more tables joined together and functioning as a single object)
(3) **QBF name** (a pairing of a form and a table or a form and a JoinDef)

Artificial intelligence techniques are used by Ingres for search optimisation based on statistics kept on all tables. A user-tunable buffer management system is also provided to keep frequently-used pages in memory on a per-user basis.

Report by forms (RBF) and Report Writer

Two facilities are provided for reporting; reporting by forms (RBF) or by the Report Writer with embedded SQL statements. The idea is to prototype the required report using RBF (which produces report writer code) and then insert SQL statements for complex reporting.

RBF is used to define and modify reports, and the REPORT option from the main menu is the execution phase. On choosing the RBF option, the name of the table to be reported on is entered. RBF will create a default report which can then be edited. Editing features include:

• Centring, deletion, column alignment
• Highlighting
• Undo (which reverses the previous operation)
• Sorting of columns in any order required
• Breakpoints (can be set at any place)
• Run-time parameters (can be entered by the user)

Once a report has been edited and saved, it can be run by using the REPORT option.

A report is created with the Report Writer by using the system editor, writing it away to the systems catalog, and then running it using the REPORT option. A report is composed of three types of command:

(1) Set-up commands, for example to control:

• how each row of data will be printed
• what happens after a break
• what happens before a break
• conditional statements (i.e. IF condition THEN action).

(2) Layout commands to:

- centre data
- set number of carriage returns to output
- set alignment of columns.

(3) Data extraction commands to:

- specify where table data is to come from
- introduce a query language command
- sort on one or more columns.

Application development using 'application by forms' (ABF)

Applications are developed in Ingres using 'application by forms' (ABF). The method employs 'visual programming', whereby an application is composed of a hierarchy of frames together with procedures, and can be called up by the use of a single command. A frame is defined as a form plus a *command menu*, where the command menu is a list of operations written in the Operation Specification Language (OSL).

The OSL gives the ability to define commands, which can then be made available from a command menu. OSL can include database access operations expressed in SQL. The language statements can be grouped into one of four kinds of blocks:

- initialisation of variables
- field activation
- menu items
- key activation.

Operation specification language statements, calls to reports, queries or programs can be included in any block. OSL operations include:

- command menu creation
- flow control between frames
- specification of database manipulation with SQL
- arithmetic computations
- user prompting
- data sharing between frames
- conditional execution.

Currently the language has to be compiled, but an interpreted version is to be made available that will facilitate ease of prototyping. The benefits of OSL are that there are fewer lines of code in the application, it provides for modular testing, there are no intermediate program variables between the database and form fields, and it allows for queries on the database.

Embedded SQL

Ingres provides the facility to embed SQL statements within the operations specification language or within a third-generation language. Six programming language interfaces (for C, FORTRAN, COBOL, BASIC, Pascal and Ada) are supported via preprocessors for embedded SQL. The source code is then compiled using the local language compiler to produce executable object code.

The OSL script is fully compiled, with the embedded SQL statements interpreted at run-time. Ingres, though, has a somewhat strange twist to this. The first time an SQL statement is used within a program, the statement is parsed, checked and then submitted to the query optimiser which determines the best method to access the database. However, if the SQL statement is met again in the same program (and under normal usage this would be very likely) the parsing and checking is not performed, so the system will perform almost as well as if it were compiled. The rationale for this line of implementation is that the database structure could be changed from one invocation to the next; however, changes to the database are not allowed while a program is being used, so it is permissible to compile the SQL statements during the running of the program.

Ingres locking

Locking is available at the table and page level. Three types of lock are supported:

(1) exclusive locks
(2) shared locks
(3) intended exclusive or intended shared locks.

Intended locks are taken on tables when exclusive or shared locking is being done at the page level within a table. Intended locks provide a useful way of determining whether it is possible to lock at the table level. Promotion of locks is supported, and deadlock situations are handled either by setting a timeout delay or by judicious coding.

Informix/4GL

Informix/4GL is a product of Informix Software (formerly Relational Database Systems) of California, USA. Informix Software produce a number of database management system products all based on the relational model and using a proprietary indexed sequential method (C-ISAM) which has become an industry standard within the UNIX community. The products are known by the extensions SQL, ESQL and 4GL. All products are available as single-user versions on PCs and multi-user versions on UNIX. The SQL and 4GL versions are also available on DEC's VAX hardware under the VMS operating system. Our discussion centres briefly on Informix/SQL and the 4GL version.

Informix/SQL

Informix/SQL is composed of the following main functional modules:

- **RDSQL** (Relational Database Structured Query Language), an enhanced implementation of the SQL language. Its functions include:
  - database creation
  - table creation and deletion
  - index checking
  - database querying.

- **Formbuild** and **Perform** respectively allow for the compilation and execution of default or custom-built forms.
- **Aceprep** and **Acego** (used respectively to compile and run reports).
- **Dbmenu**, a user-defined menu from which access to all other functions is provided.

Informix/ESQL is different from the SQL version in allowing embedded SQL statements to be placed in C programs and thus have access to Informix databases.

Informix/4GL and Informix/SQL

Informix/4GL, introduced in early 1986, is very much related to Informix/SQL. The main differences between the two are:

- The SQL provided with the 4GL version has an extended language capability.
- Lack of forms generation by 'painting' in the 4GL version.
- Language scripts have to be compiled in the 4GL version.

It is a strange marketing position, since developers would find the interpretive Informix/SQL ideal for the prototyping stage and Informix/4GL for the final version. Unlike other 4GL products (where applications are created using painted forms and tying them in with a general programming language) Informix/4GL requires both forms and programs to be entered using a conventional editor, then compiled.

Informix/4GL structure

The database data structure is created by using the CREATE DATABASE and CREATE TABLE statements found in SQL within the 4GL language script. Data definitions can easily be modified by using appropriate statements, for example ALTER TABLE.

Informix/4GL records are fixed length and serial; records added to the file are stored at the end of the file. By utilising C-ISAM, either 'unique' or 'distinct' indexes may be added. Indexes can be created on single or multiple fields, and each index can be either in ascending or descending order. The data types available are character, decimal, small integer (2 bytes), integer, small float (4 bytes), float, serial, date and money. The serial type is one for which Informix/4GL provides the next sequential number – useful for keeping track of sequentially ordered information. Each record has an 'invisible' field which is in fact the physical record number and is available to the developer.

The language

Informix/4GL is very much a language, containing a far greater proportion of procedural statements than most other 4GLs. Statements allow the following operations to be performed:

- creation of menus
- data entry and validation
- set up help messages and screens
- trap user-entered function and control keys
- set up conditional screen attributes
- create reports
- SQL statements to manipulate the database
- call C library functions.

Informix Software's rationale in supplying a system that is very much more procedural than most other 4GLs is:

(1) The non-procedural parts are terse and powerful enough to require only a few lines of code (for example when creating menus or collecting user data from forms) and handle the majority share of the application.
(2) The procedural statements allow the developer to perform operations that the designers of Informix/4GL could not predict.

The following menu-driven options are available to the application developer:

- **Module**, which allows work on program modules.
- **Form**, which allows the creation and compilation of screens.
- **Program**, which allows for the compilation and linking of the program modules.
- **Query language**, which allows use of the RDSQL language.

Forms
Screen creation in Informix/4GL is achieved by the Formbuild module.

Default screens can be generated automatically from one or more tables. However, as there is no 'paint forms' facility, form layouts are entered via an Informix-generated form specification file. Menus can be created by this method that resemble the 'ring menus' of Lotus 123. Help messages for each menu option and data entry field can be entered into a text file. The messages are automatically read and displayed at run-time when the user presses the 'help' key. Help messages can be edited without recompiling the program.

The scripts are compiled fully in a four-stage 'preprocessor, compile and link' phase. Errors encountered at this stage are inserted at the appropriate point in a temporary copy of the source code file, facilitating ease of detection and amendment. Informix/4GL modules can be compiled separately and can call each other. However, testing of the whole application requires that all modules be made available.

Run-time system

Each Informix/4GL application language script is transformed by the preprocessor to two intermediate source file types; first an embedded SQL C (ESQL/C) program and then a C program. The program is then compiled and linked using the system C compiler and function libraries. However, the SQL statements are not compiled. Instead they are passed through an interpreter at run-time for all database searches and updates.

Informix/4GL is best suited to applications that fall between the small and the medium-sized, and as a development tool to ease the migration from third-generation languages into a limited 4GL environment.

Oracle

Oracle is an SQL based product from the Oracle Corporation of California, which was founded in 1977. The product primarily comprises a database management system and an applications generator. It claims to be the first commercially available relational database management system. Oracle was originally developed for the IBM mainframe environment (VM/CMS, MVS), and has only recently been available under UNIX, followed by a PC version. A recent addition is a distributed version of Oracle, allowing users and applications transparent access to other Oracle applications on a network.

Oracle uses SQL for all data usage operations: data query, data manipulation, data definition, data control and data administration. The advantage of this is that only one language has to be learnt. Oracle SQL not only conforms to the ANSI standard but is compatible with the extended implementation in use by IBM.

Since Oracle has a mainframe origin, it was designed from the outset to manage large databases with multiple concurrent users. The major features are:

- All users share the same copy of the re-entrant Oracle code, providing minimal memory occupancy and overheads.
- Data access is handled centrally and optimised using disk caching, thus requiring the minimum number of disk accesses to retrieve data from disk.
- The data dictionary is updated on-line.
- Locking is provided at the table and record level.
- Transactions are rolled back automatically to recover from deadlocks, or if the user aborts the program.
- Users can access data from more than one database as well as from many tables in each database.

Oracle structure

At the heart of Oracle is an active data dictionary that is integrated with the rest of the system. As new tables or users are added to the database, the dictionary is updated automatically. The dictionary is itself held as data tables, and as such is available for query like any other table in the database.

All records in Oracle are of variable length, and the field types allowable are character, number, date, time and money. It provides optional indexing, using B-trees, where the indexes can be stored in either compressed or uncompressed formats. Data is itself held in a compressed form to minimise the space required by the data on disk.

On creation of a file, the developer can specify the percentage of free space that should be allocated to that file for growth (the default is 20 per cent). New records are always added to the end of the file, and not into the space set free by the deletion of records. Deleted space is used by existing records to 'grow' into, implying that a large proportion of transactions involving the creation and deletion of records will necessitate a reorganisation of the database.

Application development

An interactive environment is available for application development using a series of forms. The main tools available for the application developer are:

- **SQL*Plus**, which provides for the creation and modification of tables, and allows the user to enter and modify data values and set up ad hoc enquiries. SQL*Plus is SQL with additional features for editing, running command files, and controlling the format of output.
- **SQL*Forms** is an interactive applications generator using pop-up menus, windows and screen painting to design and modify forms-based applications. It also provides access to SQL for advanced applications. For each form used in the application, the developer is asked to specify the actions

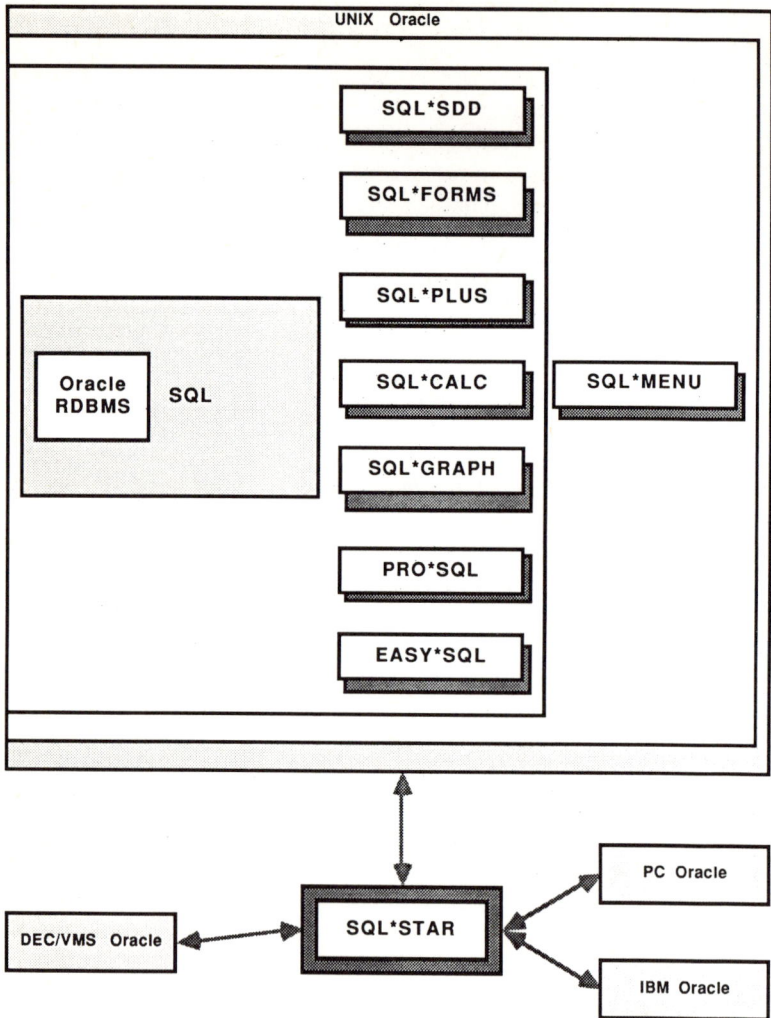

Fig. 14.5 Oracle system structure.

that have to be taken for various conditions. For complex processing the generated program can be passed to the Interactive Application Generator (IAG), which is a question and answer session.

- **SQL*Report** is a comprehensive report writing module.
- **PRO*SQL** are preprocessors for C, COBOL and FORTRAN to enable SQL statements to be embedded in third-generation language scripts. The

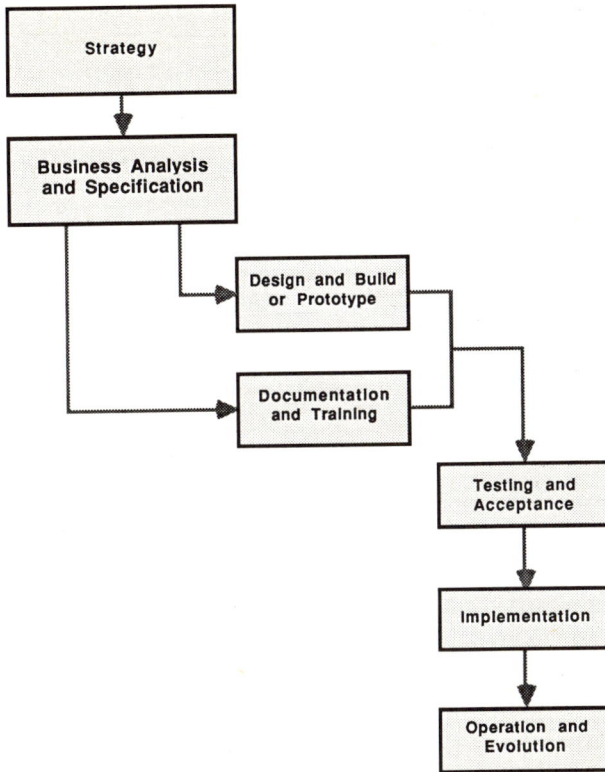

Fig. 14.6 Oracle SDD development method.

programs can then be used in stand-alone form or as routines from Oracle.

- **SQL*Design Dictionary** (SDD) is a structured system to monitor and control the development of applications at all stages of the development from initial analysis to running and maintenance.

SDD
The aim of the SQL*Design Dictionary is to assist development staff to produce a business system that meets the users' requirements. An on-line data dictionary is available to aid cost-effective development and maintenance. It provides a set of facilities to help developers during each stage in the life-cycle of a business system as defined by Oracle, namely:

- Strategy
- Analysis and business modelling
- Design
- Construction and prototyping
- Implementation and transition
- Production and maintenance.

SDD has available a number of facilities to aid the above process, including:

- Menu-driven access to interactive screens and predefined reports.
- Maintenance screens for entering, modifying and deleting data dictionary information.
- 'Query by example' and 'browse' facility using the same screens as used for maintenance, to answer questions such as:

  - Which new functions have been added to the system during the past week?
  - List the entities that are not used by any business function?

- On-line help.
- Version control.
- Glossary of terms, maintained to allow definition and accessing either by normal names or synonyms.
- Data integrity, provided by the underlying DBMS.

Tools for the user
- **SQL*Menu** is the interface through which all other services are available to the developer and user including forms, reports and commands. It is a menu environment to control and provide security in the way tasks are carried out.
- **EASY*SQL** uses a mouse and screen graphics that allow the inexperienced user to use SQL effectively simply by pointing to required operations on screen.
- **SQL*Calc** is a Lotus 123-compatible spreadsheet that allows data to be retrieved from the Oracle database. Spreadsheet cells can also invoke SQL statements.
- **SQL*Graph** provides graphic representation (bar, line, pie) automatically for data that is the result of an enquiry on the database.

Chapter Fifteen
Choosing a Fourth-Generation Language

There are literally hundreds of suppliers of fourth-generation languages, and they are available on PCs, minis and mainframes. Whether they can be classified as 'true' 4GLs – as the purists would want – is irrelevant. The primary objective of a 4GL product is to satisfy the requirements of the job in hand, and do it by decreasing the time and manpower required by a third-generation language. We repeat the definition of 4GLs that we believe to be practical and useful:

> 'Fourth-generation languages are productivity tools for the rapid development of software applications. They are tools that do not require recourse to the lengthy and formal methods associated with third-generation languages. Specifically they describe and implement what is to be done and not how it is to be done by a computer system.'

In addition some or all of the following characteristics should be looked for in a fourth-generation language:

- Non-professional programmers can obtain results using the 4GL.
- A database management system is employed.
- Programs can be created with one order of magnitude fewer instructions than COBOL; this should be a minimum criterion.
- It is very user-oriented and provides a robust and consistent interface.
- Non-procedural code is used where possible.
- Intelligent default assumptions are made about what the user wants.
- It is designed for on-line operations.
- It enforces or encourages structured code, where applicable.
- It makes it easy to understand, debug and maintain the code generated.
- Non-DP users can learn a subset of the language on a two-day training course.
- Prototypes can be created and modified quickly.

The majority of 4GLs under DOS and UNIX have these properties, but unfortunately they are not able to cope with the full spectrum of computer applications. That is the price we have to pay for the greater productivity gains that fourth-generation languages bring. As this is the case, it is imperative that a fourth-generation language is selected that fits the required application. This is repugnant to most programmers and purists, but it is a fact of life that languages of limited scope enable users to obtain the results they need quickly and effectively, whereas the traditional programming process using third-generation languages does not.

One 4GL may not be enough

It is not unusual to have more than one 4GL. At the PC level, both Lotus 123 and dBase III fall under the 4GL banner; they do different tasks and do them well. It is not unusual to have these two programs on the same machine, leaving the user to decide which is most suitable for a given task. There is also an established method of data conversion between the two programs. Higher level 4GLs, especially those linked to a database management system, come in a number of varieties and work under different environments. It should not be assumed that one 4GL will be suitable for all current and future applications. It is interesting to note that a number of multi-user UNIX-based 4GLs provide an interface to Lotus 123, so that data can be transferred from the 4GL into Lotus 123 for local processing. Such a facility helps in providing an integrated computing environment.

An understanding must be obtained – either within the DP department or in the information centre – of what each 4GL can and cannot do, as well as its suitability in different application and system environments.

Planned purchasing is necessary

Choosing a fourth-generation language is not easy; it requires the establishment of a documented evaluation method if the procurement is to be geared towards the interests of the user and not those of the supplier. The *Times* (February 1987) had this to say: 'It is quite alarming that a computer salesperson selling thousands or even hundreds of thousands of pounds worth of computer equipment will be believed and trusted to a far greater extent than the average shopkeeper or car salesman'. Very few organisations attempt a planned set of acceptance trials; instead, the suppliers' comissioning trial results are duplicated as the sole criteria of acceptance.

Our aim in this chapter is not to give the definitive purchasing plan for a fourth-generation language but rather to focus the attention of the buyer. The purchaser has to consider a variety of questions which must be answered before establishing a purchasing plan. The categories that we consider cover the full spectrum of 4GL components. The purchaser may find that it does not cover some of his special requirements, in which case a separate category should be created and questions should be asked similar to those set out here. The old proverb applies: 'one man's meat is another man's poison'. The areas covered first are those that we have found to be of the utmost significance in choosing a 4GL product, namely:

- The application
- The application environment
- The supplier
- User-friendliness
- Training.

Next, the actual details of the 4GL can be looked at, including the data dictionary and database management system.

The application

The most important set of questions should relate to the application environment. At this stage it can be decided whether or not the 4GL route is relevant to the application. Questions that have to be answered include:

- Does the application require pre-specified or ad hoc computing?
- Who will be the end users of the application; users, DP personnel, or both?
- Can the application be developed using the 4GL by the users, or will it require the skills of analysts and programmers, or a combination of the two?
- Is the application batch processing computing, routine terminal-based computing, exploratory but unpredictable computing, commercial computing, scientific and engineering computing, or complex logic computing? The majority of 4GLs are designed for applications that fit into the repetitive transaction-oriented commercial and financial environment.
- Is the application for decision support computing, and if so what categories of decision; simple, 'what if?' using spreadsheet analysis, graphical operations, sophisticated algorithms etc?
- Is it for large or low transaction volumes?
- Will the 4GL be used to build a prototype, to create the final application, or both?
- Is the application to be linked to other applications?
- Will it be linked to office automation functions like text processing, electronic mail, and office management functions?

Applications areas suitable for 4GLs

It is useful to have an idea of the sorts of area in which a 4GL can be used. We list here various applications under a number of business areas.

Marketing
Market research, demographic analysis, product tracking, market share analysis, pricing analysis, advertising tracking and analysis, marketing effectiveness studies, mail shots, etc.

Sales
Sales analysis and budgeting, customer profiles, lead management, expenses recording, commission analysis, prospect management, activity planning, etc.

Personnel
Manpower planning, staff turnover analysis, personnel directory, telephone and mailing lists, skills search, wage and salary administration, etc.

Manufacturing
Stock control, order analysis and tracking, product scheduling, absentee analysis, quality control, factory floor management, etc.

Engineering
Reliability analysis, statistical analysis, project control, etc.

Accounting
Budgeting, capital equipment tracking, expense report tracking and accounting, accounts receivable and payable analysis, etc.

Finance
Portfolio analysis, financial reporting and analysis, cost analysis, loans analysis, profitability analysis, budget preparation, etc.

Insurance
Policy proposal reporting, policy administration, claims eligibility and analysis, rate studies, etc.

The application environment
The application environment is concerned with the physical architecture of the computer system. Questions to consider include:

- Is the application part of the central computer system, or departmental?
- Is it stand-alone or part of a network (local area network or wide area network)?
- Is a distributed database facility required?
- Under whose jurisdiction is the system; DP, information centre, department or senior management?

The supplier
Supplier viability is a vital consideration in your decision to purchase a 4GL. The questions to ask should concentrate on a number of specific areas including supplier robustness, product support and product development.

- How long has the supplier been involved in supplying 4GLs and what is the supplier's long term viability?
- How many installations of the product are there in the UK, USA, and the rest of the world?
- What are the largest installations in terms of the customer, number of records, storage size, number of users?
- What is the profile category of the installations, by users and applications?
- What operating systems does the product run under, and under which manufacturers' equipment?
- How is the product distributed; directly, by software distributors, by agents, by dealers, by systems houses?
- Is support and service available locally?
- Is a telephone support line available?
- Does the supplier have facilities to correct bugs or problems quickly and easily?
- What are the sizes of the R&D and support departments respectively?
- Is on-site support available, and what is the response for on-site support?
- What are the future development plans for the product?
- What is the frequency of new releases?
- Does the 4GL have a user group and if so, how active is it?
- Can experiences and ideas be exchanged within the user group?

User-friendliness

Almost every supplier claims that its 4GL has been designed with the end user in mind. However, in practice 4GLs vary enormously in the quality of their production. Many are very difficult for end users to employ. Some are appropriate for systems analysts, some are more appropriate for professional programmers than for business analysts. It is clearly desirable to select the product which is appropriate for the user or business analyst. Developers will only use the 4GL for a short span in the life of the application; users will be needing it all day every day. It is interesting to note that the effective simplicity of the Lotus 123 screen interface has had such an effect that many 4GLs are sold with 'Lotus-like' menu structures. Some even allow the developer to generate forms with 'Lotus-like' menu options. User-friendliness is important, and the evaluation should include the following questions:

- Does the 4GL provide a uniform, robust screen interface throughout the system?
- How long will it take the user to obtain useful results – one day, half a day, or less than an hour?
- Does it provide for full self-explanatory error messages that make it clear to the user that something different is required?
- Are help screens available at all stages?

- Does the 'escape' mechanism allow the user to return to the previous operational level?
- Is the syntax easy to learn and remember?
- Is the user forced to remember mnemonics, formats or fixed sets of sequences?
- Are defaults used extensively and well?
- Can the defaults be overridden easily?
- Are split screens supported to review data, procedures, reports etc. from different parts of the application?

Training

Training is a subject that is often neglected. It is mandatory for training to be provided for the developers and users of the 4GL. The supplier should be questioned on:

- Computer-aided training; does the system provide self-teaching by actually using the 4GL on a computer?
- Are specific training courses available, and if so what are they and for what level of student (i.e. DP managers, programmers, analysts or users)?
- Are tailored, on-site courses available?
- Will each student on a course have access to a computer throughout the course?
- Are training notes available?
- What is the maximum size recommended for an effective class?
- How regularly are the courses held?
- Is the supplier the only source for the training?

Evaluation of the 4GL

Once the above has been satisfactorily completed, the purchaser can concentrate on the detailed features of the 4GL. We do not pretend to provide an exhaustive list of features to look for, since each application usually requires only a subset of all features possible. It is the purchaser's responsibility to ensure that the application requirements are met by the 4GL. One does not want to use a sledgehammer to crack a nut.

Database management system

The majority of multi-user 4GLs are intricately linked to a database management system. The DBMS should be able to define, create, store, update, archive and manage integrated data files. This includes the opening, accessing and closing of files. Some of the other main points to consider include:

- Has the DBMS been designed on the ANSI/SPARC framework for data independence?
- What type of database is it – relational, network, hierarchical? Does the DBMS support one-to-many and many-to-many relationships both directly and automatically?
- What are the disk storage requirements?
- Databases should provide for data manipulation languages to be used non-procedurally and procedurally. Does this one?
- Are there data retrieval facilities for users and developers?
- Are there database restructuring tools for database offloading, redefinition and reloading?
- Are there database administrator tools to fine-tune the database applications?
- Is there compatibility with other DBMS if more than one DBMS is used within the organisation?
- Is there an application software interface for other non-DBMS applications?
- Is there a data communications interface for geographically dispersed systems?
- Files

  - Are data compression and/or data encryption supported?
  - Does the DBMS file system allow a file to span multiple disk volumes?
  - If a file becomes full, does the DBMS automatically enlarge it?
  - How many files can be kept opened?

- Concurrency

  - What is the locking mechanism used?
  - At what level can locking be applied (i.e. database, file, record, field)?

- Is a transaction log kept?
- What are the backup and recovery procedures?

Data dictionary

The data dictionary has evolved into a facility that can represent more than the data. Many of the current 4GLs for DOS and UNIX contain record and field definitions, data types, key and indexing information, screen formats, report formats, dialogue structures, associations among many types of data, validity checks, security controls, authorisations to read or modify data, calculations for derived fields, permissible ranges for fields, logical relationships among data values, and help and error messages. The primary questions to consider include:

- Record definition; are records of fixed or variable length? What is the maximum record size and the maximum number of fields per record and records per database?
- What are the data types supported (e.g. alphanumeric, integer, float, dates, money) and how? For example can the amount (money) fields cope with the Italian Lira?
- What is the maximum length allowed for a field type and its associated description?
- For data types, what ranges are supported for data validation? What kind of value checks are available – are they simple ones and are they referential checks? (Referential checks, if supported, are of the utmost importance; for example in a customer order processing application, the user should not be able to delete a customer if there are related orders outstanding.)
- Are error messages available for failed data validation and can these error messages be user-definable?
- What access methods are supported? For example, can the primary key be indexed (ISAM), hashed (open or closed hashing), or B-tree indexed?
- Indexes

    - Can indexes be set on single, partial, combined or multiple fields?
    - What is the maximum number of indexes allowed per database?
    - Is there a restriction on the size of the indexed field or fields?

- Are pointers to primary keys supported?
- Passwords and access permissions

    - Are passwords supported and at what levels?
    - Can authorisation levels (for example 'read only') be set and at what level (database, table, record or field)?
    - Can access permissions be set for an individual user, or for a group of users?

Resource and performance

- What are the program sizes of all the modules making up the 4GL system?
- What is the minimum memory size required?
- What is the CPU throughput?
- Are tuning and optimisation facilities available?
- Is there an activity logging facility?
- Is there an independent set of benchmarks available that can be used to monitor the performance of the 4GL?
- What is the machine efficiency in a high-volume transaction processing application?
- What are the response times when the number of users doing disk-bound

transactions increases? (This is very dependent on the hardware chosen, but suppliers should have performance figures for a variety of machines.)

Forms (screen) generation

- Are forms painted on screen? If not then how are they created?
- Are default forms available for each table in the database?
- Are windowing facilities available?
- Can multi-records be displayed?
- Can help messages or corresponding help screens be set up?
- Is there control on the traversing between fields on screen?

Report generator

- Can reports be designed on screen or by line/column mode?
- Are default reports available?
- Can output be directed to storage instead of the printer?
- What are the formatting characteristics?
- Can totalling operations be performed at report production time?
- Can control breaks be set (i.e. headers, footers, etc.)?
- Is there support for a number of printers?
- Is statistical analysis available?
- Are business graphics supported (i.e. bar charts, histograms, pie charts)?
- Can a preface page be the first page of the report?
- Can summary reports be produced?

Other considerations

Some of the other features that should be examined and questioned include:

- Query language; is it based on SQL and what is its functionality?
- Query by forms; is it supported and how?
- Procedural language; is it supported, and if so what is its functionality?
- Third-generation language interfaces; are they supported and how?
- Embedded query language; is it supported?
- PC version; if the 4GL is for a multi-user environment, is there a PC version?
- PC interface; can a PC be linked to the 4GL to transfer data into, say, Lotus 123?
- System design tools; are they available, and if so, at what level of application design?
- Network; is there a local area network version? Is there a wide area network version?
- Distributed database; is there a distributed database version, and if so, is it secure and transparent to the user?

Pricing

We have left pricing till the end because, contrary to popular belief, it is not the most important issue. The majority of 4GL suppliers will have a pricing structure that is very much dependent on the size of the machine (for example a DOS version will cost far less than a UNIX version for a DEC VAX) and the number of users. Points to question include:

- What is the pricing structure?
- What are the incremental costs in adding further users?
- Is the 4GL available both as a development system and run-time system? What are the respective costs?
- What are the annual costs for support and maintenance of the 4GL?
- Is the cost of the manuals included? What are the costs for additional copies?

Fourth-generation languages are the way forward.

References

J. St. J. Bate, *Management Guide to Office Automation*, London, Collins, 1987.

J. St. J. Bate, M. Wyatt, *The Pick Operating System*, London, Collins, 1986.

J. St. J. Bate, R. Burgess, *The Automated Office*, London, Collins, 1985.

E. de Bono, *Lateral Thinking for Management*, London, McGraw-Hill, 1971.

R. Burgess, J. St. J. Bate, *Office Automation using the IBM Personal Computer System*, London, Collins, 1986.

R. Burgess (Editor), *IBM – Small and Medium Systems*, Oxford, Pergamon Infotech, 1986.

D. N. Chorafas, *4th and 5th Generation Programming Languages*, Vols 1 & 2, New York, McGraw Hill, 1986.

G. Collins, G. Blay, *Structured Systems Development Techniques*, London, Pitman, 1982.

B. Cronin (Editor), *Information Management*, London, ASLIB, 1985.

G. B. Davis, M. H. Olson, *Management Information Systems*, 2nd Edition, Singapore, McGraw-Hill, 1984.

A. Doswell, *Foundations of Business Information Systems*, London, Plenum, 1985.

C. Edwards, *Developing Microcomputer-based Business Systems*, London, Prentice Hall, 1982.

S. Hekmatpour, D. C. Ince, *Rapid Software Prototyping*, London, Open University, 1986.

IDPM (Edited), *4th Generation Languages*, Vols 1 & 2, London, IDPM, 1987.

H. C. Lucas, *Information Systems Concepts for Management*, 2nd Edition, Tokyo, McGraw-Hill, 1982.

J. Martin, *Principles of Database Management*, New Jersey, Prentice Hall, 1976.

J. Martin, *Fourth Generation Languages*, Vol 1, New Jersey, Prentice Hall, 1985.

I. Maney, I. Reid, *A Management Guide to Artificial Intelligence*, London, Gower, 1986.

T. Moto-Ora, M. Kitsuregawa, *The Fifth Generation Computer*, London, Wiley, 1985.

Opensystems Group (Editors), *Systems Behaviour*, 3rd Edition, London, Harper and Row, 1981.

A. O. Putnam, *Management Information Systems*, London, Pitman, 1977.

D. Rorvik, *As Man Becomes Machine*, London, Abacus, 1975.

M. R. Ruprecht, K. Wagoner, *Managing Office Automation*, New York, Wiley, 1984.

Glossary

access methods: Techniques used for selecting records in a file, one at a time, for processing, retrieval or storage.

ANSI (American National Standards Institute).   A highly active group affiliated with the International Organisation for Standardisation (ISO). ANSI prepares and establishes standards in a number of technical disciplines.

application generator: Software which accepts a statement of requirements (either on-screen or by file) and produces a program which fulfils the requirements without using a procedural language.

application software: A program which performs a specific task such as word processing, accounting or sales analysis, in contrast to *systems software* (e.g. the operating system) which is concerned with the effective use of a computer.

artificial intelligence (AI):   A subset of computer science concerned with the ability of machines to perform in a manner associated with human beings. This includes activities such as reasoning, learning, and self-improvement. AI implemented as a form of human/machine interface refers to the manner in which a computer can respond to English-like commands or enquiries by using human-like capacities for interpretation (e.g. the ability to examine words in context) to determine what it should do.

ASCII: American Standard Code for Information Interchange. A seven-bit plus parity bit code established by the American National Standards Institute to achieve compatibility between data services.

attribute: See *field.*

Bachman diagram: A diagrammatic design technique showing data and its structure among logical record types.

batch processing: A file updating process in which transactions are gathered and updated periodically rather than being processed immediately.

backup: A means of protecting information. It may take the form of:

(1) duplicating tapes or disks on which data is stored
(2) providing a system with an alternate power source to protect data in volatile memory in the event of power failure
(3) providing a redundant system.

block: The unit of transfer between a secondary storage device and main memory.

bottom-up: A method of development which starts from the bottom of a hierarchy and proceeds upwards.

candidate key: A field or combination of fields that uniquely identifies a record in a file; a candidate key is also a potential primary key.

catalog: Data structure that holds information about the location and representation of data.

column: See *field*.

composite key: A *candidate key* comprising more than one attribute.

conceptual view: The logical database description in the ANSI/X3/SPARC DBMS framework, also called the 'logical database'.

concurrency: The execution of two or more activities (processes, programs) in parallel.

data definition language (DDL): Language used to describe the logical properties of records and the associations among records.

dataflow diagram: A diagrammatic design technique showing a flow consisting of data which connects processes to other processes, storage or external entities.

data manipulation language (DML): An application programming language used for data access in conjunction with a DBMS.

database: A collection of interrelated data values that is represented as a number of files rather than a single file; in essence a set of integrated files.

database administrator (DBA): A person or group of people responsible for the data structure, content and supervision of a database.

database machine: Hardware designed to increase the performance of a DBMS.

database management system (DBMS): A combination of hardware and software that enables a user to employ a number of programs to access a database in an orderly fashion. A DBMS allows the configuration of a computer system with secondary storage to define, create, store, update, archive and manage a set of integrated files.

data dictionary: Contains descriptions of the entities in a database, as distinct from the raw data held in the database.

data integrity: The degree to which data values are correct in a database.

data processing (DP): The execution of a programmed sequence of operations upon data. A generic term for computing in business situations.

deadlock: A situation when a set of processes cannot proceed further because each process is waiting for a resource held by another process.

direct access: A file access method in which all records are equally accessible at any time.

direct access storage device (DASD): A data storage device that allows data in all parts to be accessed equally.

distributed database:
A database system that is located at more than one site, but which is transparent to users.

domain: In relational database theory defines a type of data item such that the contents of a column belong to the same domain for all the rows of the column.

entity: Any object about which information is held.

external view: The user's or program's view of the database as defined by the ANSI/X3/SPARC DBMS framework, also called the 'functional database'.

field: An individual item of data in a record; in relational database theory also called *column* or *attribute*.

file: A collection of data that is named.

forms generator: A method of painting forms on screen for data entry, modification, deletion etc.

indexing: A data access method for reducing storage and retrieval times by using an index to point to data.

information: The meaning derived from the relationship between symbols (words, data, etc).

interactive: Pertaining to an application in which each entry elicits a response. An interactive system may also be conversational, implying continuous dialogue between the user and the system.

internal view: The relationship between logical records and storage files as defined by the ANSI/X3/SPARC DBMS framework.

key: A field or combination of fields by which a record may be accessed.

knowledge worker: One, such as an executive or professional, who deals with information as a tool for decision making and other organisational purposes and whose productivity is not easily measurable.

locking: Technique for preventing conflicting concurrent operations on data.

logical design: The task within system design which assembles the data and processes it into a logical model of the system.

multi-tasking: Ability to process more than one process or program concurrently for the same user.

multi-user: Ability to accommodate more than one user of the system at a time.

normalisation: A design process that minimises data redundancy and updates anomalies in an integrated database.

paging: A process associated with virtual storage in which memory is divided into pages that can be transferred to disk during processing operations so that effective memory capacity is vastly increased.

physical design: A task within system design during which the logical model of the system is tailored to meet the physical constraints set by the hardware and software to be used.

physical view: Describes how data is stored on physical storage in the ANSI/X3/SPARC DBMS framework.

primary key: A field or combination of fields that uniquely identifies a record in a file.

query by forms (QBF): A method of querying a database by the use of predefined forms.

query language: A non-procedural language with which users of a DBMS can perform operations on a database. In relational database theory also called the 'relational calculus'.

record: A single entry in a file; in relational database theory also called a 'tuple' or 'row'.

redundancy: The presence of duplicate information and/or equipment.

relation: A collection of semantically related information also referred to as a 'table'.

relational algebra: A procedural language to specify the operations to be performed on a database without reference to access paths.

relational calculus: See *query language.*

relational database: A database model which removes the constraints regarding the logical relationship between data by reducing all the data to a set of relations (tables).

report generator: A method of specifying formatted ad hoc reports either on-screen or via a sequence of pre-written report language statements.

rollback: A DBMS recovery technique. On database failure it aborts active transactions and then attempts to recreate the state of the database prior to failure.

row: See *record.*

SQL (Structured Query Language): A relational database query language developed by IBM.

table: See *relation*.

time sharing: A technique for sharing the time of a computer among several jobs, implemented at the operating system level. The rapid switching between jobs gives the impression that users are accessing the services of the computer simultaneously.

top-down: The design of a system or program by first creating components and their relationships at a high level of detail and then proceeding to design them, each to the next level, and so on to the lowest.

transaction: A single coherent action on a file or database. A transaction might be;

(1) an insertion of a new record

(2) a deletion of an existing record or

(3) a modification of an existing record.

tuple: See *record*.

Index